GLASNEVIN
HOUSE

GLASNEVIN HOUSE

A Sense of Place

VIVIENNE KEELY

The
History
Press
Ireland

First published 2014

The History Press Ireland
50 City Quay
Dublin 2
Ireland
www.thehistorypress.ie

British Library Cataloguing in Publication Data.
A catalogue record for this book is available from the British Library.

ISBN 978 1 84588 839 8

Typesetting and origination by The History Press

CONTENTS

Abbreviations   6

1   Mobhi to Mitchell   7
2   The Lindsay Family and the Sacred Heart Sisters   31
3   Holy Faith Sisters in Glasnevin House   53
4   Convent Chapel: Construction,
    Liturgical Furniture and Decoration   71
5   The 1901 Census: Village and Convent Community   87
6   The Site Takes its Present Shape   109

    Afterword by Ralph Bingham   125
    Notes   129
    Index   141

Abbreviations

BMH	Bureau of Military History
CRO	Companies Registration Office
DDA	Dublin Diocesan Archives
DIA	Dictionary of Irish Architects
HFA	Holy Faith Archives, Glasnevin, Dublin 11
IARC	Irish Architects Archive
IB	*Irish Builder*
MAV	Mount Anville Archives, Sisters of the Sacred Heart
NAI	National Archives of Ireland, Bishop Street, Dublin
NL	National Library
NGI	National Gallery Ireland
ROD	Registry of Deeds, King's Inn, Dublin

1

Mobhi to Mitchell

ARCHAEOLOGY

Generations of Holy Faith sisters walked the banks of the River Tolka to a small grotto known as Mobhi's Cell. Whether it is an evocation of the spirit of early Irish monasticism or the memorialisation of an historic figure, the naming of Mobhi's Cell in the grounds of Glasnevin convent ensures that the first question to be posed about the lands at Holy Faith Convent, Glasnevin, centres on their relationship to the monastic site. The early medieval ecclesiastical settlement at Glasnevin is associated principally with St Mobhi, who died around 544. Colmcille, Comgall of Bangor, Ciarán and Canice were among the fifty or so monks and students reputed to have congregated around Mobhi in Glasnevin. Legend has it that, in response to a prayer of St Canice, the students' cells, situated south of the Tolka, migrated north of the river to St Mobhi's church.[1] Legend aside, St Mobhi's church, abutting the Bon Secours Hospital, is thought to have been the centre of the early monastery and the area surrounding it is designated a zone of archaeological interest.

The legacy and spiritual traditions of the early monks were evoked by Margaret Aylward, foundress of the Holy Faith congregation, when the sisters moved to Glasnevin in 1865:

> Our fathers in the faith, the early saints of Ireland, knew the power of beautiful scenery to attune their minds to religion. Hence we find the ruins of their abbeys and monasteries beside the river's bank ... It is not too much to say that St Brigid's new home at Glasnevin is one of those spots fashioned by the Almighty Architect for religious exercises.[2]

Those who look to the archaeological record for confirmation of the oral and early literary tradition will be disappointed. The excavations, carried out in preparation for housing developments and institutional expansion in the vicinity of the zone of archaeological interest, have failed to establish a firm connection to the early monastic site. The Bon Secours Hospital site promised much, since a number of burials had been discovered there between 1914 and 1956, giving rise to the hope that a burial site associated with Mobhi's monastic settlement might be uncovered. However, in a series of investigations spanning 1989 to 2005 nothing was found to indicate the presence of an earlier burial ground. The only remains of interest were those associated with the eighteenth-century occupation of the hospital site when it was Delville House, home of the Delany family.[3]

This stone, situated outside the Bon Secours Hospital, marks the place where Mobhi's monastery is thought to have stood.

By far the most significant find in the area was from the 1998 excavation at Holy Faith Convent, Glasnevin. This was a line-impressed tile with a six foil in-circle pattern identical with tiles from Christ Church Cathedral, St Mary's Abbey, St Saviour's Friary, Wood Quay and Kildare Cathedral. Thought to be of fourteenth-century manufacture, the tile was recovered from the topsoil, indicating that it been disturbed from its original location. The archaeologist, Richard O'Brien, concluded that the 'tile fragment would suggest some ecclesiastical activity in the general area of the site, presumably connected with the medieval church of St Mobhi'.[4] It is important to note that this conclusion relates only to late medieval activity, as a fourteenth-century artefact is surely too distant in time from the sixth century to sustain a link between St Mobhi and the convent site.

The eighteenth-century occupation of the convent site was confirmed by other excavations on the convent grounds. In 1799 a survey carried out for George Putland had marked and named on a map an outhouse, offices and farmhouse at the Old Finglas Road/Ballygall Road end of the property. The 2001 excavation, associated with the sale of convent land for the building of the apartment complex now known as Addison Park, revealed remnants of an eighteenth-century farmhouse consistent with the position of the farmhouse on the 1799 Survey map. Similarly, a dwelling house marked on the 1799 Survey at the Ballymun Road end of the convent site is consistent with the location of a brick floor and wall exposed in a 1996 investigation. These remains related to the house or outhouses built by Sir John Rogerson or Hugh Henry Mitchell in the early to mid-eighteenth century, parts of which became Glasnevin House.[5]

The new centre in the convent grounds lies just over 300m to the east of the zone of archaeological interest associated with St Mobhi. The 6-inch Ordnance Survey map of around 1838 shows an earthwork, circular in shape, approximately 20m in diameter and situated about 50m from the proposed new centre. Prior to the construction of the centre, an excavation was carried out in 2010 to confirm or not the presence of an earthwork, and it was hoped that this excavation would also throw some light on the configuration of the formal garden laid out by Hugh Henry Mitchell around 1760.[6] However, the few artefacts uncovered from two trenches were of recent origin except for a fragment of a mottled-ware tankard from the eighteenth century. The excavation revealed no evidence of an earlier earthwork, no artefacts of archaeological significance, no association with the early monastic settlement and no indication of the eighteenth-century formal garden.[7] In sum, no link from the convent site to the early monastic settlement of St Mobhi can be established from the archaeological evidence. The fragment of floor tile from the 1998 excavation near the present Marian House in the convent grounds is a tenuous link to fourteenth-century monastic activity in the area. Archaeological evidence can neither establish nor corroborate a link from the convent site to the early monastic settlement.

It is emotional geography rather than archaeology itself which supplies a framework for weaving together the strands of place that make up the Glasnevin convent site. A sub-discipline of ethno-archaeology, emotional geography, focuses on 'the sensory and affective qualities of place as shown in the character, arrangement and interrelations of place and such elements as people and heritage'. In so doing it attends to 'oral traditions, relationships and kinship, moral obligations, narratives, daily life and ritual performance'.[8] In her writings, Margaret Aylward fashioned this sense of place by aligning the practice of the holy ancients to the project of her day by connecting historical figures, for example, Daniel O'Connell whose memorial lies in the neighbouring Prospect Cemetery, to her pressing educational mission. Thus she constructed a narrative of spiritual kinship in the service of her educational mission, a narrative buttressed by the religious routines of daily conventual life, and one which supported the development of the network of St Brigid's Schools and promoted Glasnevin as a centre for the rituals of pilgrimage and processions.

DEVELOPMENT OF GLASNEVIN LANDS

For more than 800 years Christ Church Cathedral was integral to the development of the Holy Faith lands at Glasnevin: from 1178, when the lands were part of a large tract granted to the priory of the Holy Trinity by Laurence O'Toole, Archbishop of Dublin, to 1941, when the fee simple was purchased by the Sisters of the Holy Faith from the descendants of Bishop Charles Lindsay. Bishop of Kildare and dean of the Christ Church Cathedral Chapter, Lindsay was one of the previous owners of Glasnevin House. In the twelfth century, Holy Trinity Priory had acquired most of the lands of Glasnevin, Gorman (later Grangegorman) and Clonkeen (later Kill of the Grange). Grants outside Dublin, including some in County Down from John de Courcey and Hugh de Lacy, made the priory the most richly endowed religious house in Ireland. Its preeminence was reflected in the taxation assessment of the early fourteenth century, which rated the priory's Dublin holdings at £182 19s 8d against the rating for St Mary's Abbey at £80 2s 1d.[9] In 1300 there were only eleven canons of St Augustine in Holy Trinity, barely sufficient in number to administer the priory and its large tracts of lands.

The priory roll of this time, around 1326, shows that there were thirty-eight individuals on the Glasnevin grange paying rent to the priory. Of these, nine were women, of whom only one was designated a widow. Rents ranged from 27s to 6d. In addition to payment of rent at stipulated times, tenants had to perform labour, but the requirement was minimal compared with that in England. Farmers were required to plough, harvest, hoe, and make up hay. Several also had to supply fowl at certain times. Geoffrey Fynche had to give three hens at Christmas or 3d, and others were required to give one hen. The account roll gives some information about occupations: a brewer, a smith, a turner and a driver of a plough team are mentioned, and John Fox would work as a cottager. Other positions recorded include the chaplain, the clerk, and the chamberlain of the lord.[10]

The priory depended on the farms of the grange for a steady supply of some of the produce it required; wheat and oats were the most commonly grown crops, followed by barley, rye, beans, peas and leeks.

Nicholas Chamberlain was the bailiff of the manor of Glasnevin. The position of bailiff was one of

importance and Nicholas was paid 50s ½d for managing
the husbandry. Once a fortnight the prior would visit the
farm and would sit at table to enjoy the farm produce,
supplemented by treats such as almonds, oysters, and ale
supplied by the bailiff.[11] Ale for the prior is recorded
against the account of the Glasnevin grange in several
entries in the account roll record of 1338; in January
3d was paid; on the second Friday of Lent 4d was paid;
shortly after Easter the same amount was paid for ale.
There are two entries for wine for the prior in Glasnevin:
2d was paid for wine on Easter Monday and the same
amount in the following week. At this time a gallon of
wine cost 6d.

After the Dissolution of the Monasteries, Glasnevin
and its farms continued to be a source of revenue and
food for the reconstituted chapter of Christ Church
Cathedral and its dean.[12] Two seventeenth-century
surveys indicate the extent, divisions and sub-lettings of
land in Glasnevin. The Francis Survey and map shows
the two largest holdings as the Seven Farms, mainly south
of the Tolka, and the Great Farm, mainly north of the
Tolka and to the east of the village. The farms are shown
as parcels within a greater area of land, and it is there that
the name of Putland appears: 'Mr Putland's Demesne'.
The Putlands, John and his son George, were significant
figures in the development of the suburb of Glasnevin
and the convent site. According to the Civil Survey of
1654–56, the land owned by Christ Church Cathedral
in Glasnevin extended over 400 acres. It was leased in
lots. By far the two largest lots were the Seven Farms,
comprising 190 acres, and the Great Farm, comprising
125 acres. Three smaller lots were Gracott's, comprising

38 acres, Foster's 31 acres and Gough's 16 acres.[13] The land's resumption by Parliament and its subsequent resale enabled Sir John Rogerson to purchase extensive holdings of land in Glasnevin in 1703. The arrival of this wealthy merchant was a boon to the area. He set about improving the village and its environs, thus laying the foundations for Glasnevin as a location of choice for the emerging villa-style of housing soon to be favoured by the wealthy of Dublin. Rogerson had built for himself the house which would become Glasnevin House, the original part of the Holy Faith Convent.[14] The house was situated at the end of Glasnevin village facing the Naul Road (now the intersection of Old Finglas Road and Ballymun Road).

HUGH HENRY MITCHELL

The tangled chronology of ownership and occupancy by lease and sub-lease of Glasnevin House is difficult to negotiate, but a firm anchor is the deed of 1774 which confirms leases already enjoyed and those being executed in that year. Hugh Henry Mitchell's purchase of the dwelling house and garden, together with 5 acres, stables, coach house and outhouses from Sir John Rogerson for £130 15s is confirmed.[15] Mitchell was well known in Dublin society as a banker and Member of Parliament for most of the 1760s, firstly representing Castlebar, County Mayo and later Bannow, County Wexford. Another player in the development of Glasnevin Demesne was John Putland, whose stepfather was Richard Helsham, co-owner of Delville with Patrick Delany for some years.

In 1734 Putland had received from Helsham an interest in 428 acres of land around Glasnevin, previously owned by Christ Church Cathedral. For a sum of £6,000, Putland received Gough's Farm of 16 acres, Dean's Farm of 21 acres, Seven Farms of 190 acres, Great Farm of 125 acres and Draycott's Farm of 38 acres. This was a large outlay of money for a young man; £6,000 in the 1730s would be equivalent to £778,200 today.[16] The acreages involved in Putland's purchase are close to those set down in the Civil Survey of 1654–56. Putland's newly acquired lands extended to the present Westmoreland Bridge, popularly known as Cross Guns Bridge, and included the Botanic Gardens as well as Glasnevin village. It appears that George Putland was living in Glasnevin House around 1748.[17] The Glasnevin Demesne and its 47 or so acres, which later came into Holy Faith ownership, was composed of Mitchell's original 5 acres and a portion of Putland's lands. On his new estate, Mitchell built a house which incorporated part of the earlier Rogerson building, commissioned some of the major improvements in interior alterations and decoration and carried out extensive landscaping, all of which works were continued during the occupancy of the house by his son, also named Hugh Henry Mitchell. Putland and his son George continued to be the ground landlords until at least 1799.[18]

The Mitchell house and gardens attracted favourable attention in Glasnevin, then an area 'remarkable for the large and elegant improvements made by many gentlemen residing in and near the place; especially the house and gardens of Hugh Henry Mitchell, Esq. The demesne is highly improved.' Mitchell was said to have had 'great skill in horticultural design. In his time the gardens and demesne of Glasnevin House became celebrated and attracted everyone from the viceroy downwards.'[19] Recent scholarship reiterates the view that Mitchell was responsible for improvements to Glasnevin House and its impressive rococo interiors.[20] Women of the period were known to occupy themselves with gardens and landscaping. Lady Louisa Conolly of Castletown House and Emily Fitzgerald, Duchess of Leinster, provided support for the view that for women 'landscape design was a social and environmental responsibility and this concern for health and happiness coincided with their interest in pedagogy'.[21] Unfortunately Hugh Henry Mitchell's wife does not speak to us from the sources, so her involvement in the layout of the walks of Glasnevin Demesne is unknown. Mitchell, either father or son, planted the cedar of Lebanon, some branches of which have perished so that its wonderful natural symmetry, captured in Brendan Scally's sketch, is no longer visible. From time to time a small branch blew down in a storm, but the most dramatic loss occurred during a fierce storm in September 2003, when a complete section of the tree fell away.

The favourable assessments of Glasnevin House and its demesne reflect the genteel and elegant eighteenth-century lifestyle of those who chose to reside in Glasnevin in order to enjoy the benefits of fresh air while remaining within easy reach of the capital. Animating this society was the lively Mary Delany (1700–88), the second wife of Patrick Delany, the owner of Delville, Fellow of Trinity College and later Dean of Down. On 11 acres, on a slight rise, Delville could boast well laid-out walks with elm and evergreen oaks, an orchard with orange and

other fruit trees, and a large kitchen garden. Its high wall
was erected mainly to safeguard the herd of deer. Like
the main Glasnevin residences of the eighteenth-century
gentry, Delville was neither town house nor country
house, but rather a villa. This style of housing had
quickly become the envy of those confined to the city,
as Mrs Delany reveals in a letter: 'Now everybody is going
out of town, the sun shines, and they come in swarms
to take leave and bask in the sunshine which the smoke
of the city will not allow.' The frieze of the temple in
the Deville garden bore the words *'fastigia despicit urbis'*
('it looks down on the roofs of the city'), thus reinforcing
the sense of separation and lofty grandeur which the
residents of the villas espoused.[22] Like Glasnevin House,
Delville was situated on the north side of the Tolka,
the preferred side for villa owners because it commanded

The south-facing façade of Mitchell's Georgian house.

both mountain and sea views. A sketch by Mary Delany
in the National Gallery of Ireland shows the view from
Delville across Dublin Bay to the Dublin Mountains, with
the wall of Delville in the lower foreground. Some artistic
liberties have been taken with the topography to achieve
the desired effect.[23]

The cedar in Glasnevin convent grounds.

Delville House itself was architecturally unremarkable for its period. Mary Delany described her residence as one of two storeys with a high patio ascended by six steps. There were five windows in the front of the house which featured a hall 36ft by 12ft with Doric entablature in stucco. Mrs Delany described 'a very neat stone stair-case, well-finished with stucco'. Although the interior plasterwork, executed mainly by Dublin artists, was favourably viewed by Curran, his description and the two plates illustrating the plasterwork support the conclusion that Delville's plasterwork was not as impressive as that in Mitchell's house up the road.[24] Following a custom of the time, Mrs Delany used shellwork as imitation stucco in the decoration of the ceiling of her chapel.[25] No such imitative work was evident in Glasnevin House. The Delanys put more time and resources into the development of their pleasure garden and walks, in which the influence of Alexander Pope could be detected. Although fashionable in design and benefiting from continued improvement, the garden was the subject of a slightly satirical poem, the sense of which is captured in the couplet 'and round this garden is a walk, no longer than a tailor's chalk', a reference to the grand design of the garden and buildings, thought to be somewhat pretentious for an estate of its size.[26]

It is not surprising then that it is the garden which is highlighted in Mary Delany's artistic representations of Delville. Her five works, in ink, graphite and wash on paper – *The Beggar's Hut*, *The Evergreen Grove*, *The Cold Bath Field*, *The View of Swift and Swans Island* – showcase elements of the planted and built garden environment.[27] When, many years later, Delville 'that haunt of ancient peace' came to be sold, it was suggested that the finding of type in the vault of the summerhouse indicated that clandestine printing had been carried out there around 1842.[28] By then Mary Delany had long since departed the scene, having returned to her native England on the death of her husband. There, living in Windsor, she enjoyed the friendship and largesse of King George III and Queen Charlotte.

There is evidence to suggest that Mrs Delany would have been intrigued by Margaret Aylward's sisters and their way of life had she been able to meet them a century later. The nuns with whom Mary Delany was acquainted lived a contemplative, cloistered life. She describes meeting a Miss Crilly, who was 'a nun professed' and who was brought to visit her in Delville House. Indeed Mrs Delany returned the visits, calling on Miss Crilly at her 'nunnery in King Street', where there was a 'very handsome parlour' in which guests were received without the presence of a grille. The fact that nuns 'in this country have the liberty of going to see relatives and particular friends' amazed the Delville patronne.[29] Although Mrs Delany would have liked to develop her friendship with Miss Crilly she thought that others in her circle would have been suspicious of her motives. We can be sure that she would have been more than surprised to meet Margaret Aylward's sisters walking from Glasnevin to the schools in inner-city Dublin.

GLASNEVIN HOUSE

Architectural assessments of Glasnevin House range from a Palladian eighteenth-century villa to a nondescript nineteenth-century house. *A Guide to Irish Country Houses*, published in 1988, summarily dismisses it as 'a plain two storey c. nineteenth century house with a single storey high-roofed wing at right angles'. Another view elevates the house to 'an early eighteenth century villa with a pediment extending over the whole front in the full Palladian tradition so that the Knight of Glin considers it almost certainly by Sir Edward Lovett Pearce'.[30] With Richard Castle (Cassels), Pearce was one of the two preeminent exponents of Palladian architecture in Ireland. He is responsible for Castletown House, familiar to many Holy Faith sisters who lived in Celbridge, County Kildare. Pearce's use of brick lent elegance to, and gained acceptance for, this building material.[31] For one driving up Glasnevin Hill in 2014, or walking down Ballymun Road, the ensemble of Glasnevin House requires close inspection to justify its Percean origins or, if they be denied, then its eighteenth-century date. Small wonder then that the attribution of Glasnevin House to Pearce was not universal among architectural historians. It does not appear among the nineteen buildings 'in some way connected to Pearce' identified by Maurice Craig in 1996, but finds a secure place in Jeremy Williams's study of further candidates for such attribution. Williams unequivocally attributes Glasnevin House to Pearce: 'This is a Pearcean villa added to an earlier farmhouse.'[32]

The former north-facing entrance to Glasnevin House is clearly a recessed entry between two wings. The western one is little changed but the eastern wing has been modified interiorly and built over externally, so that the symmetry of wings and recessed entry has lost its original expression. Moreover the entrance door itself has been removed and has been replaced by a low-silled window with pedimented Ionic frame which Williams claims 'is a modest version of one of the aedicular archways that frame Pearce's forecourt to his Parliament House'.[33] The modifications to the entrance and hall were carried out in around 1874, when Margaret Aylward extended the convent. This is attested to, somewhat ruefully, by one of the residents of the convent at that time, Sr Rose Gaughren:

> A large addition had to be made and some of the former building, although a magnificently built old structure occupied by the Sacred Heart nuns for about ten years before Miss Aylward got it, had to be thrown down, chiefly a beautiful hall leading to the front door. This was done in order to connect the new building with the old without leaving an unsightly gap between them.[34]

The ground-floor, north-facing room, with original chimneypiece remaining and dated to mid-eighteenth century, served as a chapel for the Sacred Heart sisters. The new community also used it as a chapel, and it was there that the first Holy Faith sisters to make public vows did so on 15 August 1869. The group included Margaret Aylward, Rose Gaughren and Agnes Vickers. This room was later used as the Holy Faith novices' refectory and, in recent times, has become the vesting room for the priest celebrating Mass for the nursing home residents, as a supplementary dining room for special events and, occasionally, as a training room for the staff of Marian House nursing home.

The cantilevered stone service stair and the main mahogany staircase are situated in the west wing and are adjacent to each other but counter-directional.

At the top of the main staircase are three archways. The left archway leads to the oldest part of the house, past the service stair to a small north-facing, one-bay room with original window in place. This arrangement is matched on the mezzanine below. The central arch leads to a suite of three rooms, two south-facing, built over the reception rooms below, and one north-facing. The right archway leads to a south-facing two-bay room and adjoining it a one-bay room. This was at one time the bedroom of the foundress, Margaret Aylward, and the room in which she died.

The explanation which makes most sense of the architecture of the present Glasnevin House, which presents two storeys on its southern side and two storeys plus mezzanine on its north side, is that the south-facing parts of the house were additions, and joined to the Rogerson house by the mahogany staircase which is beside the service staircase. Such encasing of one house, or part of one house, by another was not uncommon. Elements of the Rogerson house may be seen in the barrel-vaulted basements. The added elements include, on the ground floor, the two reception rooms with splendid stucco ceilings. Original joinery, chimneypieces and windows complement the extensively decorated plasterwork.

While the surviving upper window of the north-facing older section of the house has thick glazing bars with small panes, the windows of the south-facing ground-floor reception rooms have finer glazing bars, which style became fashionable from the 1750s. Mrs Delany of Delville embraced the fashion and was quite proud of her newly installed sashes, 'made in the narrow way, which makes them much pleasanter'.[35] Finer glazing bars and larger panes made for greater light in the interior, which would have been appreciated by all, but particularly by an artist of the calibre of Mary Delany. The panes of the ground-floor windows of Glasnevin House are arranged in the nine over six pattern which was to become typical of Dublin Georgian houses. Those of the upper-floor windows are in a more modest six over six pattern, consistent with their status as rooms of lesser importance than the reception rooms beneath them. For each window in the large three-bay reception room there are upper and lower sets of shutters. Two bands of mouldings decorate the window surround. Here some overpainting has dulled the crispness of the moulding.

All the internal doors of this section of the house are common Georgian six-panel doors. The door cases have two sets of mouldings. Both rooms feature elaborate overdoor treatments, praised by the Knight of Glin: 'The woodwork is of the highest quality, particularly the overdoors carved in high relief with flower swags suspended from nails. The overdoors clearly relate to the work of John Kelly in Dublin and may be attributed to him.'[36] The decoration of the three internal doors of the large reception room and the two doors of the smaller reception room are identical, with a deep frieze of floral garlands, arranged symmetrically and surmounted by a cornice composed of waterleaf moulding, dentil moulding, fillet, and a crown of waterleaf moulding.

The chimneypiece of the smaller two-bay reception room is of neo-classical design in white marble with inlays on the frieze and jambs. The frieze is centred by a large white marble tablet carved in high relief with a Grecian urn, its pleated drape knotted at each side and falling away. A leaf design corbel on the jambs leads to a framed shell with seven flowerets falling the length of the pilasters, a delicate proportion achieved by placing the largest flowerets in the centre. The overall effect of the chimneypiece in the adjacent large reception room has been somewhat marred by the mysterious disappearance of the white marble tablet in the central frieze. It depicted a woman at a loom.

The highly regarded plasterwork of Glasnevin House finds its most eloquent expression in the three-bay reception room, complemented by the decorated walls of the stairwell. In the reception room the central ceiling panel is left untouched by any decoration, but

The elaborate cove in the large reception room in Mitchell Georgian House.

The impressive overdoor. It is thought to be the work of John Kelly.

the deep cove is a riot of acanthus foliage, pendants of fruit and flowers. Large C-scrolls with trailing ends arc around the room. Stairwells are recognised as the loci of impressive Irish rococo work and Glasnevin House's stairwell is no exception. On the north and south walls are large cartouches of acanthus scrolls, C-scrolls and rocaille with oversized garlands and daisies, strongly reminiscent of those at Russborough.[37] The German influence stemming from Roscher and Preisler has been noted by McDonnell and Marrinan.[38] Although not a common feature of Dublin Georgian windows, a large Venetian window breaks the western wall of the staircase. Here the cartouche of acanthus, C-scrolls and rocaille reappears. The mahogany staircase itself is open-string with turned balusters and a decorative bracket at each tread. The handrail ends in a very fine volute.

The smaller reception room is decorated in a style different from its neighbour. The ceiling is divided into twenty-one compartments, mostly undecorated. The ornamentation is confined to the compartment dividers, decorated with daisies and roses, though the large outer frames contain floral elements gathered in strings of miniature shells and continuing the motifs of the reception room and staircase. This compartmentalised treatment is reminiscent of the designs of Sir Williams Chambers and suggests a date of around 1760, which is consistent with the date suggested for the rest of the stucco work. However, the eating parlour of Delville, dating from around 1729, boasted a compartmented ceiling with decorated frames, so neither the suggestion of the reception room's derivation from Chambers nor the date of 1760 is conclusive.[39]

As the Knight of Glin and James Peill have noted, the plasterwork of Glasnevin House is after the manner of the Lefranchini brothers, in whose work the acanthus leaf was a dominant motif. Although the same motif dominates the plasterwork of Glasnevin House, its author had not been definitively established.[40] In recent times the suggestion that St Peter's Stuccodore is responsible for the stucco work in Mitchell's eighteenth-century house has gained acceptance. The term 'St Peter's Stuccodore' is assigned to the artist responsible for the decoration of St Peter's church, Drogheda. Working in late Baroque style, this unknown craftsman from Europe was active with his troupe in Dublin and noted for his use of the auricular cartouche in the tympana, a design first used in Ireland by Sir Edgar Lovett Pearce. Stylistic similarities between the plasterwork of Russborough House and St Peter's, Drogheda, whose plasterwork was carried out between 1749 and 1752, have led to the conclusion that St Peter's Stuccodore executed work at Russborough.[41] This artist is now recognised as the second hand at work in Russborough after the Lefranchini. A recent study of the Glasnevin plasterwork concludes that, based on similarities and modifications to the Russborough House design, the author of the Glasnevin stucco work and the second hand at Russborough are one and the same person.[42] Therefore if the second hand at Russborough is St Peter's Stuccodore, he is also the author of the Glasnevin House plasterwork. This conclusion pushes the date of the Glasnevin stucco work to the 1760s.[43] Regardless of the precise date, the quality and execution of the decorative plasterwork of Glasnevin House shows it to be anything but a plain two-storey nineteenth-century building.

The contribution, if any, of the well-known builder Alexander Strain to the Glasnevin convent site is difficult to ascertain. It has been suggested that he built the 1901 chapel but it can be established that W.H. Byrne was the architect for the chapel, with James Kiernan the contractor.[44] A very brief sketch of the history of the convent from 1865 states that Alexander Strain built the 1874 extension to the Georgian house, now the main convent building.[45] That view has to be discounted, because Strain was born in 1873 or 1874 in County Armagh, the son of the builder, Robert Douglas Strain, whose presence in Dublin is listed in Thom's Directory for 1907.[46] In 1874 Robert Douglas would have been 28 years old. He cannot be definitively ruled out as the builder of the 1874 convent, but it is unlikely that such a commission would have been entrusted to one so young and relatively inexperienced.

Glasnevin House is on the list of Protected Structures and is entered in the National Inventory of Architectural Heritage.

2

THE LINDSAY FAMILY AND THE SACRED HEART SISTERS

CHARLES LINDSAY AND
GLASNEVIN HOUSE

Early in the nineteenth century the villa known as
Glasnevin House and its lands were purchased by
Charles Dalrymple Lindsay (1760–1846). Third son
of the 5th Earl of Balcarres, Lindsay had arrived in
Ireland as private secretary to the Earl of Hardwick,
Lord Lieutenant of Ireland and a relative by marriage.
Lindsay had been educated at Glasgow University and
was Snell Exhibitioner in 1779, a prize which allowed
him to undertake postgraduate studies at Balliol
College, Oxford.[1] He married Elizabeth Fydell in 1790
and was appointed vicar of Suttonton, Lincolnshire,
in 1793. Elizabeth and Charles had four living children:
Elizabeth, the first-born, named after her mother;
Charles, the eldest son, named after his father; and the
two youngest boys Thomas and Philip Yorke. Sadly,
twin boys and a daughter had died in infancy. Elizabeth
Fydell died in 1797 after only nine years of marriage
and having borne seven children. The following year,
Lindsay married Catherine Eliza Coussmaker, with
whom he had two sons, George Haywood and Henry.[2]
A few years after his arrival in Ireland, Lindsay was
appointed Bishop of Killaloe and Kelfenora, and was
installed in his bishopric on 13 November 1803. Barely
six months later, in May 1804, he was translated to
Kildare as Bishop of Kildare and dean of Christ
Church, the two positions being held jointly at that
time. His short sojourn in his County Clare diocese
was caustically reported: 'In 1803 he was appointed to
this See, but in the year following he abandoned it for a

Bishop Lindsay's prayer stool. (Courtesy of Glasnevin Archives)

better, that of Kildare.'[3] His eldest son, Charles, was to
follow in his footsteps, becoming an archdeacon in the
diocese of Kildare.

Lindsay chose to live in Glasnevin, which historically
was connected with Christ Church Cathedral through
property holdings and individuals who were prominent
in the affairs of the Church of Ireland and in civil
administration. Since the incumbency of George Stone
in 1734, the deans of Christ Church had declined to live
in the house reserved for the dean in Fishamble Street.[4]
When Charles Lindsay moved into Glasnevin House,
he was about 44 years old with at least five children,
ranging in age from Henry, aged 3, to Elizabeth, aged 13.
The rooms, halls and grounds of Glasnevin House rang
with the laughter and cries of children playing.

Little is known of the domestic life of the Lindsays
in Glasnevin House or of how they managed the
estate or furnished the house. They could have
purchased crockery from Wedgewood's showrooms in
Sackville Street or the upmarket Donovan's glass and
china shop on George's Quay. The newly constructed
Westmoreland Street provided another possibility in
Samuel Alker's china and glass shop. Elegant furniture
could have been made by Lewis and Anthony Morgan,
cabinetmakers in Henry Street.[5]

It appears that Lindsay had already owned a house
in Glasnevin before acquiring Glasnevin House and
Demesne. He donated it to the Irish Harp Society
and in 1804 the artist Eliza Trotter painted the walls
of the reception room in bas-relief images of the harp.
The location of this house is unknown, despite a query
in *The Irish Book Lover* in 1930 seeking its location, which

elicited no published response.[6] It is possible that the donation of the house was made in 1804, the same year in which Lindsay became dean of the chapter of Christ Church and Bishop of Kildare. The newly appointed dean of Christ Church would have needed a commodious and elegant residence befitting his episcopal status. That Lindsay was conscious of status became evident when in 1807 the Royal Canal Company advertised a small piece of land, presently the rose garden in the National Botanical Gardens. Lindsay thought that the acquisition of this parcel of land would provide a more fitting and ornamental approach to his house, apart from the obvious advantage of its situation at the bottom of the hill! He sent the advertisement to Forster at the Botanic Gardens, who suggested that the Dublin Society purchase it and lease it to the bishop at £25 per year.[7]

The year 1811 augured well for the Lindsay family, with the marriage of the eldest Lindsay daughter, Elizabeth Frances, to Compton Domville of Templeogue House and Santry House, who had an estate of over 6,000 acres in County Dublin. The marriage took place under special licence in St Mobhi's Church, Glasnevin, on 21 October 1811.[8] Happiness quickly turned to tragedy when Elizabeth died the following year, possibly from complications in childbirth. The baby lived and was christened Compton Charles Domville after his father and maternal grandfather. Created a baronet in 1815, Compton Domville remarried and lived to be 84. Bishop Lindsay was to know the loss of another child the very next year when his second eldest son from his first marriage, Thomas, a lieutenant, was killed in

June 1812 at the Battle of Vittoria – a victory for the British forces against Napoleon but another tragedy for the Lindsay family. With the death of Thomas, five of Lindsay's seven children with his first wife, Elizabeth Fydell, were dead.

The bishop was active in the care of the needy in Glasnevin and Finglas and in the provision of education in Glasnevin, acting as patron of the parish school, 'the Inkbottle'. Established by Patrick Delany of Delville in 1727, the school lurched from one financial crisis to another, as might be expected since its funding depended on sporadically held subscriptions. From 1817 efforts were made to put the school on a surer financial footing with the opening of a new subscription, headed by Mrs Lindsay. Ten years later, more regular financial support was ensured by means of an annual donation from parishioners in addition to the subscription list. The school was put under the patronage of Bishop Lindsay, and a more rigorous governance structure was introduced.[9]

In 1818 there had been a severe outbreak of typhus in Dublin, so virulent as to cause the Cork Street Fever Hospital to admit 3,000 patients in one month. In February 1819, from the Gresham Hotel, Dublin, Lindsay wrote a covering letter signed Charles Kildare to accompany the Report of the Glasnevin and Finglas Board of Health. Hints of a proprietary and self-promotional tone are evident beneath the nineteenth-century epistolary style and rhetoric. He refers to 'our' Glasnevin and Finglas Board and avers that 'we have greatly reduced our number of sick' though giving due credit to the 'skilful and indefatigable attention' of Robert Walsh, the Church of Ireland curate of Finglas, who lived in Glasnevin, and Dr Hart (the latter substituting for Dr Walsh, brother to the curate, who was himself ill). In pointing to 'a circumstance of fearful import, namely that twenty eight heads of houses, counting in Finglas a population of one hundred individual, are without any kind of employment,' Lindsay stressed the need to create work so that men could afford nutritious food for their families. However, in asserting that the situation in Glasnevin was better than that in Finglas, he did not hesitate to assume a large measure of the credit himself:

> You must not deem me a boaster, because truth obliges me to observe that there would be like enumeration of distributes [sic] from Glasnevin had I not taken care to make work for the old and weakly people. I must add that I am no loser by it and get value for my encouragement.[10]

This claim was by way of justification for the appeal for additional funds made in the Report in 1820. The fever returned to Finglas, causing Lindsay to opine that 'it may revisit all those who have previously been affected'.[11]

Despite his involvement in education and health in the Glasnevin area, Lindsay had to face public allegations of maladministration in the Diocese of Kildare. To the Undersecretary of Ireland, W.H. Gregory, he denied 'any small glaring neglect of duty' in relation to the returns of resident and non-resident clergy to Dublin Castle, though acknowledging previous errors. The following year, 1819, the disaffection of others over proposed realignment of parish boundaries in the diocese of Kildare, rather than allegations of maladministration, obliged Lindsay to write to the Chief Secretary, Charles Grant, defending his actions in separating or merging parishes in the diocese, when unfavourable reports appeared in the Dublin and London papers.[12] For a great part of his time as Dean of Christ Church Lindsay was involved in prolonged wrangling over the issue of non-residence of canons who held several posts and their consequent absence from the church services in which they were required to participate. His chief adversary in this regard was Richard Graves, but the issue cut closer to home and Lindsay was at pains to insist that his son, Charles, who was both archdeacon in Kildare, where he had a parish, and curate in Monkstown, in the diocese of Dublin, was assiduous in his attendance at Sunday services in Monkstown. Lindsay clashed too with Archbishop McGee over the latter's rights of visitation, but this dispute was amicably resolved. However, it is incontestable that Lindsay made a sustained effort to introduce discipline into the affairs of the Chapter of Christ Church.[13]

The late 1820s brought great change to the Lindsay household. The bishop moved from Glasnevin House in around 1828, and the Carmelite Brothers took up residence, having arrived there from Fairview. Known as the Carmelite Brothers, it appears that this was a lay group of Carmelite tertiaries supervised by a layman, John Young. They were to remain in Glasnevin House until 1849. At the outbreak of cholera in 1827 Lindsay had set up a temporary hospital in the grounds of

Glasnevin to help deal with the epidemic. O'Doherty suggests that the Carmelites may have been assisting in the temporary hospital.[14] In the middle of the cholera epidemic, in 1828, the elder son of Bishop Lindsay's second marriage, George Haywood Lindsay, married Lady Mary Catherine Gore. George and his son, Lt-Col Henry Gore Lindsay, were the Lindsay family members who had most to do with Margaret Aylward and the Sisters of the Holy Faith. Catherine Gore was the daughter of Col William John Gore whose family were extensive land owners. The tithe applotment book shows Col Gore as the owner of The Turrets in 1828, which was a house in Claremont Avenue taking its name from its tower-like central block, built in Jacobean style by Sir John Rogerson around 1710.[15] Later, the bishop's son, George Lindsay, built a house adjoining The Turrets and gave the name Glasnevin House to the ensemble after the original home, which was in the ownership of the Sisters of the Holy Faith from 1865.

It was to The Turrets that Bishop Lindsay moved in 1829. The move to a house owned at the time by his brother-in-law strengthens the claim that the bishop may have been in some financial difficulty. It may be presumed that the Carmelite Brothers were paying rent in return for their occupancy of Glasnevin House. Glasnevin was owned by Lindsay personally, whereas his other income was derived from rent on the holdings of the dean of Christ Church. Charles Lindsay was the last cleric to hold conjointly the offices of Bishop of Kildare and dean of Christ Church. The diocese of Kildare was voided in accordance with the Church Temporalities Act 1833, the terms of which did not take effect until the death of the incumbent in 1846, at which point Kildare became part of the diocese of Dublin and the dean of St Patrick's Cathedral also became the dean of Christ Church.[16]

At the time of the cholera epidemic, Glasnevin Catholics belonged to the Roman Catholic parish of Clontarf which, along with the Church of Ireland parish of Glasnevin, came under the auspices of the Dublin Union of Clontarf. The responses to a questionnaire of 1832–35, penned by Revd W. Walsh, Roman Catholic priest, afford some insight into the parlous condition of the poor of that area and reveal a link with the Lindsay family. The document confirms that a great part of the area of the Union was covered with trees because of the number of private estates and villas, the largest being that of Marino and the Santry holdings of Lindsay's former son-in-law, Sir Compton Domville. However, Walsh was less well informed about Glasnevin than about other places in the Union. He was aware of three dispensaries in the Union operating by subscription and of a fourth in Glasnevin, but did not know how it was operated. He mentions a widows' house at Glasnevin, but it is more likely that he was referring to the new almshouse. With regard to the general condition of the people, Walsh states that potatoes were the staple diet of the poor, relieved occasionally by some coarse oaten bread. A great many people were half-clothed and their beds were without blankets. The two greatest evils, nominated by Walsh, were the absentee landlords, who contributed nothing to public institutions or subscriptions, and the wide availability of alcohol through thirty-two licensed premises and fifteen or so unlicensed outlets. With considerable acuity, Walsh stressed that the availability of a Savings Bank would be a great help to the working poor.[17]

Although Bishop Lindsay had left Glasnevin House he retained the ownership of the property, and the Tithe Applotment Books 1823–37 continued to show Glasnevin House and Demesne with intermixed lands in the ownership of the 'Lord Bishop of Kildare'.[18] Lindsay continued to take a personal interest in his property. Before Easter in 1840 he was obliged to inform Revd Mr Armstrong that 'palms' would not be available from the usual source, the yew trees in Glasnevin. A storm in January 1839 had severely

The Yew Walk in the convent grounds.

affected the yew trees with 'many branches destroyed to the extent that to denude them further would be to their detriment'.[19] The yew walk in Glasnevin Demesne is a twin of the yew walk in the Botanic Gardens on the other side of the Tolka, the river which forms a boundary between the properties. Thought to have been the idea of Thomas Tickell, the date of the planting of the yew walk, or Addison's Walk as it is called, in the Botanic Gardens is uncertain, nor can the identity of the person responsible for it be confirmed. A photograph taken in 1897 shows an avenue of quite mature trees while the photograph of 1981 appears to show little change.[20] Both photographs are practically indistinguishable from the companion yew walk in the grounds of Glasnevin convent.

Bishop Lindsay's daughter-in-law, Lady Mary Catherine Gore, was sister to Philip Yorke Gore, 4th Earl of Arran, through whose agency some seeds and plants were provided to the Botanic Gardens. Arran himself was a keen gardener and, as a member of the diplomatic corps, was in contact with John Tweedie, a retired Scottish gardener and botanist, living in Buenos Aires. Through this network, consignments of seeds from South America were sent to Ninian Niven, curator of the Botanic Gardens, the first consignment arriving in 1834.[21] Lord Arran was known to visit the gardens occasionally, bringing seeds and plants, and it is highly likely that a visit to the gardens would also include a visit to his sister in Glasnevin and perhaps the gift of some plants from South America. The Lindsay family maintained their contacts with the men closely associated with the Botanic Gardens, an association perhaps attributable to their Scottish connection;

all these men were Scots and the Lindsay family's roots were in Scotland.[22] The connection with Scotland remained very much alive, evidenced when Bishop Lindsay brought dairymen from Scotland to Glasnevin to staff the dairy he had established, which used the most modern methods. Importing workers was sufficient to alienate the local workers, who retaliated by dubbing Lindsay the 'Buttermilk Bishop'.[23]

GEORGE HAYWOOD LINSDAY AND GLASNEVIN

A few years after the move to The Turrets, Bishop Lindsay's third son with Elizabeth Fydell, Philip, died in Cape Province, South Africa in 1832. His death left Charles, the archdeacon, as the only surviving child of the first marriage and one of three sons living at the time of the bishop's death in 1846. Bishop Lindsay bequeathed his Glasnevin estate not to Archdeacon Charles but to his eldest son from his second marriage, George Haywood Lindsay. Charles inherited his father's manuscripts with instructions to burn those he thought should be burned, a gold repeating watch made by Wrigley and a miniature portrait of his mother, Elizabeth Fydell. The bishop's widow, Catherine Eliza Coussmaker, was bequeathed her husband's books as well as those books she 'was possessed of at her marriage'. Financial provision was made for the widow in the form of an immediate payment of £1,000 and an annuity of £350.[24] Catherine outlived her husband by seven years, dying aged 92 on 21 May 1852. She was buried in Glasnevin.[25]

Griffith's Valuation of 1848 shows George Lindsay's holding at Glasnevin Demesne at 41 acres, 2 roods and 15 perches with a primary valuation of £165 7s. The buildings' primary valuation was £90. Lindsay held other lands in Glasnevin: 35 acres at Claremont; 33 acres at Hampstead Hill; 49 acres in Ballygall; 44 acres in Bankfarm; over 21 acres at Violet Hill Great and over 23 acres at Violet Hill Little, a further 23 acres at Walnut Grove, a small parcel in Glasnevin and interests in Donnybrook. These extensive holdings made the Lindsays one of the major landowners in Glasnevin at the time of the Great Famine. George Lindsay was a member of the Glasnevin Vestry Famine Relief Committee and proposed donating a piece of land for the erection of fever sheds, an offer which the committee had no hesitation in accepting. Lindsay was not present at the meeting, his offer being conveyed by one, M. Dunne.[26]

George Lindsay was also interested in practical applications of agricultural science which would ensure a better potato crop and to this end sent a paper on the cultivation of the potato to the Famine Relief Commission. The paper had been written by Alexander Campbell, a gardener employed under the National Schools Commission and one whose knowledge was rated highly by George Lindsay: 'He has been a very successful competitor in flowers and vegetables and possesses a superior knowledge of growing the potato.'[27] Alexander Campbell went on to own a nursery at 12 Ballymun Road, then Church Hill, later occupied by the Craigie family, who operated a well-known dairy on the premises.

SACRED HEART SISTERS
OCCUPY GLASNEVIN HOUSE

In 1853, seven years after the death of Bishop Charles Lindsay, the Lindsay heirs sold Glasnevin House to the Sisters of the Sacred Heart. Described in the Memorial of the Conveyance of the Deed as the 'Mansion House', with its 47 acres it was sold through the agency of a Mr Thomas Scully, whose daughter Julia was a member, and nine years later superior, of the Glasnevin community. Glasnevin was the third foundation of the Sacred Heart sisters in Ireland after Roscrea and Armagh. It was Cardinal Cullen who had encouraged the sisters to establish a foundation in Armagh and it was he who encouraged them to come to Dublin. The sisters were convinced that the expansion of their order in Ireland necessitated a house in the capital city, and Cardinal Cullen's move from Armagh to Dublin made it a fortuitous time to establish a house there.[28] Mother Croft, who had been the founding superior in the other houses, was appointed to lead the new foundation and to find a suitable location for it. She and Mother Scully were the first Sisters of the Sacred Heart to arrive in Glasnevin, followed the next day by Sr Rose. Their arrival was recorded:

> It was on the 7 October 1853 that the village of Glasnevin first saw the nuns who, it was rumoured, had bought the house belonging to the family of the late Anglican Bishop Lindsay and intended to settle there. It was not an imposing body of people who drove through the streets of Glasnevin that day ... secular dress was still necessary whilst travelling and the little band who had set out that

morning from Armagh, the most Protestant city in the north of
Ireland, were laden with packages for the new foundation and
somewhat weary and bedraggled.[29]

The sisters' opinion of the house and its environs was
favourable but measured. One account records that
the house selected, though relatively small, had the
advantage of being built on a hill, surrounded by acres
of well cultivated land, and was generally considered to
be one of the 'prettiest spots in the neighbourhood'.[30]
The complete site comprised 46 acres, 3 roods and
28 perches, and was composed of four parcels of land:
the house itself, standing in 8 statute acres; a second
parcel of 3 acres and 3 perches; another parcel of 3 acres;
and the last portion of 32 acres, 3 roods and 25 perches.[31]
The ample acreage certainly compensated for the small
size of the house.

A couple of weeks after the sisters' arrival, the first Mass
was said in the small chapel on 23 October 1853, an event
which merited mention in the journal of the community:
'On this day which was a Sunday the holy sacrifice of
the Mass was offered for the first time in the house by
the reverend Father Superior of the Lazarists. From
that day the holy sacrifice of the Mass was offered on
Sundays by one of these religious.' Permission to have the
Blessed Sacrament reserved in the chapel was given by
Cardinal Cullen after the official blessing of the convent
23 December 1853.[32]

The sisters operated two schools, a secondary
boarding school and a primary school. The first boarder
was received 23 December 1853, but the school began
slowly enough, with only ten pupils at the end of the

first seven months of operation in July 1854. The new school year began with a healthier enrolment of thirty pupils which had increased to fifty-seven by the end of the school year. The boarders were housed in the convent. A new primary school, the 'poor school', was built and enrolled eighty children, some as young as three. It was well patronised and the sisters had great hopes for it: the children were eager to learn, they benefited from the care given to them and good relations existed between sisters and parents. In the view of the sisters, the Catholic inhabitants of Glasnevin were quite poor; in fact, their poverty so great that the sisters were convinced that food and clothing were the best presents that could be given.[33]

Some Catholic lay women in Glasnevin village had formed themselves into a group known as the Congregation of St Joseph. They visited the sick, advised the priest of those who were seriously ill, acquired the necessities for the administration of the sacrament of the sick. From their own resources they raised money to have Masses said for the dying and the dead, contributed to the St Vincent de Paul orphanage and established a library.[34] The sisters were busy acting as spiritual guides for these women, making the convent facilities available to them and to the Children of Mary, who used the chapel for retreats, meetings and prayers, at the same time as they themselves were receiving postulants, conducting a novitiate, and operating their two schools.

No wonder that the limitations of the house became critically evident; it was simply too small to accommodate the sisters and the increasing number of boarders and novices. Enrolments had increased steadily and so many young women were coming to join the sisters that space was fast becoming an issue – one which could no longer be ignored. The available accommodation was so crowded that novices who had completed their first year in Glasnevin had to be sent to Paris for their second novitiate year. A stark choice faced the sisters: expand or move. The decision to leave Glasnevin and seek another property was difficult and had a few false starts. The community journal records that different opinions were held in the community about staying or leaving but all were agreed that more space was needed. A site at Mount Anville was considered but when it first became available, the price was beyond what the sisters could afford, so they decided to extend in Glasnevin. An architect was commissioned and plans were drawn up.

Matters were complicated by gossip and scare-mongering. It was put about that the illness among the boarding school pupils was caused by the proximity of the school to Prospect Cemetery and enrolments dropped off. Friends of the sisters tried to prevent further encroachment of the cemetery and enrolments increased for some time until they were adversely affected by yet another extension of the cemetery which brought it even closer to the convent lands. The last straw was a mild outbreak of smallpox which affected the pupils, among whom was Cardinal Cullen's niece. Enrolments plummeted to the extent that there was little hope of regaining lost confidence and so the decision to move was final.[35] Ironically, many years later, in 1911, an advertisement for the school featured its 'unusually healthy position'.[36]

Mr Thomas Scully was instrumental in negotiating a more favourable price for Mount Anville from the owner, Mr Dargan. The price was accepted and the contract for the purchase of Mount Anville was signed on Wednesday 19 May 1865.[37] According to their custom, the sisters decided to exhume the remains of their deceased sisters from their Glasnevin convent cemetery and reinter them in the new property at Mount Anville.[38] Four professed sisters, one novice, and one aspirant lay sister had died in Glasnevin in the period 1853–65. One was Mother Eliza Croft, the first of the Glasnevin community to die. Another was a past pupil of the school, Catherine Chadwick, who had developed lung trouble while in France completing her novitiate. In the hope of recovering her strength in her native air, she was sent back to Ireland but succumbed to her illness and died, aged 20, in 1861. On 27 September 1865, Canon Ford presided at a ceremony of blessing immediately prior to the exhumation of the six bodies.[39]

Notwithstanding the persuasive reasons for moving to Mount Anville and the years of discernment and false hopes, the sisters were sad to go: 'it was not without sorrow that the house at Glasnevin was given up. The people of Glasnevin had endeared themselves to the nuns by their faith and generous love of the Sacred Heart. The Holy Faith nuns, a Congregation not long established, presented themselves.' The departing community consoled itself with the thought that the arrival of the new community would ensure that their house would 'remain a home and centre for the people of Glasnevin'.[40] This new congregation had its genesis five years before the Sacred Heart sisters took up residence in Glasnevin, when, in 1851, Margaret Aylward founded the Dublin City branch of the Ladies of Charity of St Vincent de Paul.[41] In collaboration with others, including Fr John Gowan CM and the laywomen Ada Allingham, Marianne Scully and Frances Murray, she set up St Brigid's Orphanage, conducted on the boarding-out system and a work which was to receive Cardinal Cullen's approbation in 1859.[42]

Cullen was a great supporter of Margaret Aylward and her ideas on faith, family and a suitable environment for the raising of children. He was to become an equally keen supporter of the St Brigid's Schools.[43] In 1861 the first St Brigid's school was opened in Crow Street. The development of the Holy Faith congregation went hand in hand with the development of the schools of St Brigid, which were established for the education of poor children. A quasi-religious life was being lived by Margaret Aylward's helpers in Eccles Street. Margaret Gaughren, then resident in Eccles Street, recalls the plain black dress, black bead collar, chenille veil on head, black straw bonnet for school and black shawl on the street. With Fr Gowan officiating at the simple ceremony, Margaret and her companions received new names and, shortly afterwards, received large brass crosses and a black cashmere cape. These were worn for the first time on St Patrick's Day 1863.[44]

In subsequent visits to France, during which she visited spas to take the waters for various debilitating medical conditions, Miss Aylward observed practices in religious congregations which she later introduced to her own congregation or which confirmed for her the wisdom of her earlier decisions. From Aix-les-Bains she wrote to Ada Allingham concerning the dress of the religious she had seen in France:

> I suppose the dress of all [the sisters] except the grand is rather like ours, black dress, black cape & small silver cross in front & on the head a close black cap with a fringe made two fingers deep of a thin bonnet shape like any home laced bonnet shape you might buy & add it to a black night cap.[45]

Visiting the poor in their homes was important for Margaret Aylward, and she was particularly interested to observe and take heart from congregations with similar ideas. She visited a group of Francisan sisters in Aix-la-Chapelle and noted:

> … the object of the institute – attending and relieving sick poor in their houses, begging alms for them and for themselves and eating the same as the poor eat, but not the sick poor as they must get something better. They do this all gratuitously. Their vows are perpetual. They go to the streets alone.[46]

Going to the streets and eschewing enclosure was fundamental for Miss Aylward's future congregation. In fact on the streets of Dublin, they were sometimes known as the 'sisters of the streets'.

3

HOLY FAITH SISTERS IN GLASNEVIN HOUSE

ARRIVAL

An anonymous sketch of the early history of the congregation confirms that lack of space in Eccles Street convent was the impetus for searching for another property and also testifies to the numerous, though unsuccessful, attempts to find a suitable alternative: 'Great pains were taken and arrangements nearly completed several times but some obstacle would turn up to prevent the place from being taken'.[1] Tantalisingly the author of the historical sketch gives no information on the location of the several sites whose purchase did not come to pass.

Finally the Glasnevin property was secured and at 3.45 p.m. on the afternoon of 10 October 1865, Margaret Aylward of Eccles Street had 'granted, assigned and made over' to her Glasnevin House and approximately 47 acres, 3 roods and 25 perches.[2] The other parties to the transaction were for, the first part, Julianna Scully and Hermandine Bastid, both of Glasnevin, and Marianna Scully, then at Rome; for the second part Bernard William Delaney of Queen's County; for the third part Margaret Aylward. Both Julianna Scully and Margaret Aylward are identified as spinsters.

Once in possession of the title, and at Cardinal Cullen's suggestion, Margaret Aylward wrote to the Holy See in 1866 seeking recognition for the new congregation.[3] Just as Cardinal Cullen's hand was in the coming of the Sacred Heart sisters to Glasnevin, so it was also in the purchase of the house by Margaret Aylward. For her, Glasnevin was unlike any other convent in the congregation, most of which were to be close to the schools they would serve in fidelity to Margaret Aylward's dictum that the sisters 'live in an ordinary house attached to the school, and go to Mass like the rest of the Faithful'.[4] The particular place of Glasnevin in the life of the congregation and in the emergence of St Brigid's Schools is the subject of this chapter.

In 1865 the Congregation numbered a mere eighteen sisters: Margaret Aylward and her sister Scholastica Fagan, Ada Allingham, Rose Gaughren, Magdelen Maguire, the Vickers sisters Agnes and Mary Ann, Teresa Graves, Monica O'Brien, Brigid Meade, Margaret Markey and seven postulants. Margaret Aylward initially did not reside in Glasnevin, preferring to reside in Eccles Street, but she visited Glasnevin every day to attend to the business of installing the community in their new home. She came to live in Glasnevin in the late 1860s.

According to Rose Gaughren's history, the day after the departure of the Sisters of the Sacred Heart, the first group of Holy Faith sisters, five in number, moved to Glasnevin, with the larger group arriving the following year. However, the anonymous account states that the first sisters moved in on the very day that the Sacred Heart sisters departed. Both accounts agree that, on night the sisters moved in, there was a great thunderstorm and, as they had no beds set up, they were obliged to sleep in mattresses on the floor. The first general viewing by the sisters of the new convent took place on Sunday 15 October 1865: 'All the sisters went for the first time to see the place. They were disarmed with the beauty of the grounds and with the large and beautifully built rooms, ceilings etc.'[5]

At this time the property consisted of Glasnevin House, a gate lodge, four workmen's houses at the Violet Hill end of the site, a coach house and farm buildings, grounds in some state of neglect, a house which became known as St Michael's and the school built by the Sacred Heart sisters, which is now Aylward House. In use as a boys' school was a structure of unknown date called the Tin Shed. In 1877 Margaret received a letter from George Lindsay stating that he owned a plot of ground opposite the convent property on the other side of the river and that he thought it would be advantageous for her to buy it. After protracted negotiations Margaret succeeded in purchasing it and a bridge over the Tolka was constructed 19 July 1877.

The Lindsays remained prominent landowners in the environs of Glasnevin. In fact, it was not until 1941 that the ground rents attached to the convent and schools were bought from the representatives of the Lindsay family. In June 1941 the trustees of the will of Henry Gore Lindsay decided to auction the fee simple rents of the Lindsay properties in Glasnevin, as well as those of Walnut Grove, Iona and Ballsbridge. Mother Eilzabeth Kelly wrote to Archbishop McQuaid, seeking permission to buy the fee simple and enclosing the cutting of the newspaper advertisement. McQuaid replied giving permission 'in so far as it pertains to me'.[6] Thus the Lindsay family's connection with Glasnevin House and Demesne came to an end 141 years after it began.

GLASNEVIN SCHOOLS

A school building to the right, inside the main entrance to Glasnevin, built by the Sacred Heart sisters, was improved in 1868 with the addition of a shed and outdoor toilets.

The sisters renamed it St Brigid's and operated it as a private school. When the second-generation boarding school was built in 1901, the private primary school became a girls' national school and remained so for many years. School accommodation was extended in the 1960s by a separate building known as St Joseph's, which provided additional classrooms, a cookery room and principal's office. Eventually increasing enrolments necessitated an even larger building with better playing facilities.

In 1976, St Brigid's National School migrated up the Old Finglas Road to its present site. The new building was designed by D.J. Munden, son of Patrick Munden, architect of St Mary's Secondary School. The old primary school was converted to offices for the central administration of the Holy Faith sisters and is known as Aylward House. St Joseph's was used as an educational centre for the travelling community. The widening of Old Finglas Road resulted in the demolition of the gate lodge and bicycle shed.

The boarding school, Our Lady of the Angels, got under way in 1873 in the convent. The Georgian suite of rooms was variously used as classrooms and dormitories. In March 1873 a Mr Lewis was paid £26 to erect a partition separating the classrooms from the dormitories. New crockery and utensils were purchased: twenty-six cups, saucers, breakfast plates, thirty-two dinner plates, knives, forks and tea spoons.[7]

Like the Sacred Heart sisters before them, the Holy Faith sisters soon realised that the conditions were too cramped. It was clear that more room was needed to accommodate the growing number of sisters and provide for the boarders, and so in 1874 Margaret

The convent alongside Georgian House.

Aylward had the main convent built. It was an extension
of the original house, a simple building of three storeys
continuing westwards from the Mitchell house with
south-facing frontage. A long, single-storey, brick-faced
building was erected to be used as a dairy, laundry
and drying room. The main convent was funded by
Margaret Aylward from her personal resources. In 1903
a spacious kitchen was built in what had been a yard.
It was built over a well, which was rediscovered, with
water still flowing, in a later building project.

To promote the school, 500 school prospectuses
were published by Brown & Nolan in March 1873.
Advertisements placed in *The Irish Times* in July 1874 cost
16*s* and those in the *Freeman's Journal* in October 1875
cost £3 19*s*[8] A half-year's pension for boarders in
1876 was £10 and for the same period extra tuition
in French was £1, in drawing £2 and in music £2.
Milk, butter, vegetables and eggs were supplied by the
convent for the boarders and reimbursement was made

to the convent account. As the sisters were running a small farm, it is probable that the dairy produce and eggs were from the farm's cows and hens and that the vegetables were home-grown. Tea, cocoa, sugar and rice were purchased. The beverage payments were £14 2s for tea and 10s 6d for cocoa. Birmingham butchers supplied the meat. Local dressmakers benefited: the April 1876 ledger shows payments for the making of dresses for five pupils, two at 2s and three at 3s.[9] The sisters charged with particular care of the boarders in the early days were Evangelist Hayes and Stanislaus O'Keefe.

A comparison of two early advertisements for the school is instructive. The first, in August 1874, appeals to 'persons who are anxious to find in Ireland a convent in which education is provided for a moderate pension'. The intention was that children might be 'improved in their education, and fitted for Home Duties or Conventual Life'. The proposed curriculum offered religious instruction, spelling, writing, ciphering, grammar, geography, history, English composition, needlework and domestic duties. French and music were optional and tuition was additional to the regular subjects for which the yearly pension was 20 guineas to be paid as half-yearly instalments. The situation of the school is highlighted, 'beautifully situated with a Demesne of 48 acres, about a mile from the city'. Ease of transport from the city was suggested 'conveyance by Onmibus, from the Bank of Ireland, every hour'.[10] Reference to home duties and conventual life had disappeared when, in 1880, the boarding school was advertised in the *Catholic Ordo* (Yearbook) for 1880:

Boarding school for young ladies under the patronage of His
Grace the archbishop of Dublin and the direction of the Rev. John
Gowan, CM. The Sisters of Faith offer a first class education to
young ladies in their new establishment. Beautifully situated on the
banks of the Tolka ... with conveyance by tram car from Nelson's
Pillar every twenty minutes. Terms – 20 guineas per anum. Music,
French, Drawing and Dancing extra. Further particulars may be
had at the convent.

It is interesting that no mention was made of Margaret
Aylward, the foundress, who was still alive in 1880, and
noteworthy, but not surprising, that Fr Gowan was named
as the director of the school. From the very beginning
of the Holy Faith schools, Fr Gowan had supervised
the religious instruction given in the poor schools and
overseen the curriculum studied by boarders and younger
sisters alike. The yearly pension for boarding and tuition
remained unchanged.

Also noteworthy is the appearance of the tram and
its promotion as an incentive for students to travel to
Glasnevin. The tramline to Glasnevin had opened
only four years earlier in 1876 and was then operated
by the North Dublin Street Tramways Company which
was eventually subsumed into the Dublin United Tram
Company. At first it was a horse-drawn tram ending
at Tolka Bridge but, in 1899, it was electrified and was
extended up the Washerwoman's Hill (Glasnevin Hill),
to the terminus right outside the convent. The school
was quick to capitalise on this development, featuring
it in advertisements the very next year: 'Conveyance
by electric tram to convent gate every few minutes.'[11]
The tram operated until the outbreak of the

Second World War in 1939. From 1919 onwards the Glasnevin tram number was number 19, later the number of the bus service which served Glasnevin until withdrawn by Dublin Bus in 2011.

GLASNEVIN'S ROLE IN THE MISSION OF ST BRIGID'S SCHOOLS

The purchase of Glasnevin was key to Margaret Aylward's strategy for promoting the work of St Brigid's Schools, which were fast developing. Glasnevin's 47 acres in a splendid setting not 2 miles from the city centre promised to serve key elements of the mission of the schools and the formation of the students who attended them. Although the house at 46 Eccles Street was and remained for many years the home of St Brigid's Orphanage, it could not be considered as the future headquarters for a congregation in which the main work of an increasing number of sisters would be in the city schools and who would therefore not be directly involved with the work of the orphanage, which was not a residential facility but a fosterage service. Moreover, a group of religious women seeking canonical recognition as a religious congregation needed a large mother house where the religious life of the fledgling congregation could be nourished, a novitiate established and arrangements for the governance of the institution set in place. So, on one level, the initial impetus for the move to Glasnevin was a pragmatic response to an emerging organisational need for an embryonic religious congregation.

On a deeper level, Glasnevin became an integral part
of the educational mission of Margaret Aylward. Ever
an activist and deeply committed to the education of
the children of St Brigid's, the acquisition of Glasnevin
gave Margaret Aylward the freedom to turn her mind
to the development of the schools network. Crow Street
had been established in 1861 and Great Strand Street
two years later. To these were added Jervis Street (1870),
Clarendon Street (1870), Kilcullen, County Kildare
(1873), Skerries (1875), Celbridge, County Kildare (1878)
and Mullinavat, County Kilkenny (1879). The opening
of schools in the inner city and beyond continued in the
1880s with Dominick Street (1884), the Coombe (1887)
and Little Strand Street (1888). Miss Aylward died in 1889
and in the decade after her death, schools at Clontarf,
Haddington Road, Finglas and Kilcoole, County Wicklow
were established. Standing at the head of this network of
schools was Holy Faith Convent, Glasnevin.

Clearly, for the sisters working in the inner-city schools
of Park, Crow and Clarendon Streets, and the Coombe,
Glasnevin would be a place of spiritual refreshment
and healthy living which would sustain them for their
labour in the unsanitary conditions of the slums of
Dublin. Very soon the site of Glasnevin's impressive
natural setting and strong Celtic spiritual associations
were exploited by Margaret Aylward and Fr John
Gowan for their particular view of Catholic education in
nineteenth-century Ireland.

In 1831, with the cooperation of the various Churches,
a national system of State-sponsored primary education
was introduced. It was to be non-denominational but
with separate religious instruction provided. Most schools

run by religious congregations aligned themselves with the new system under the national board of education. However, Margaret Aylward was determined that her schools would not participate in the system of education supervised by the National Board. This firmly-held conviction was based on her fear of proselytism, a fear well founded at the time and supported by her experiences with the Irish Church Mission. Miss Aylward's schools remained outside the National Board, for above all she feared interference in religious instruction. She was convinced that in a Christian education religion should pervade the entire climate of the school, rather than being merely unit of the curriculum among others. She was adamant that St Brigid's Schools would accept no money from the national board and vigorously maintain their independence. Her initial educational philosophy was a mix of religious and nationalist conviction.

She and Fr Gowan missed no opportunity to capitalise on the monastic traditions which associated the lands of the mother house with the early Irish monks: 'Apart from everything – away from all and in the midst of hermitages, grottoes, waterfalls, where the saints would love to dwell and as St. Canice, St. Kieran and others trod this ground it is well to touch the sod that bore them.'[12] But the monastic traditions of Glasnevin were not to be harnessed for the spiritual comfort of the individual sister; the aim was always mission oriented. The two elements of the beauty of the setting and early Irish monastic associations were woven together in the service of a multi-pronged educational project: education of the poor, schools for the middle classes and teacher formation:

Here in this retreat at Glasnevin those fathers of the Irish Church made their preparation for the apostolic work that God had destined them for; and going forth, full of the spirit of God, they became the lights of the western world. Here then St Brigid will rest, and, if it please God, religious teachers will grow up under her patronage that will devote themselves to the instruction and sanctification of the poor children of holy Ireland.[13]

Aylward drew a parallel between the early monks and the teachers of her day, both nourished by the beauty of Glasnevin and both committed to the mission of Catholic education. The network of St Brigid's Schools was catering for poor primary-school-aged children. Glasnevin was to have a particular function in the development of Aylward's drive for the middle classes and teacher formation. While never departing from the founding aim, the education of poor children, Margaret Aylward and Fr Gowan were sensible of the advantages to this project of opening schools for children from better-off families. As early as 1866, the year after moving into Glasnevin and before the establishment of the convent boarding school, Margaret Aylward wrote:

If it please God we shall not confine our efforts to the teaching of the poor, but found schools for higher classes, the profits of which shall be applied to the maintenance of schools for the poor – our chief care being the poor, and our principal object the defence of the Faith.[14]

These schools for the 'higher classes' or 'middle schools' – both terms were used by Margaret Aylward – were to be opened when parents requested a Catholic education for their children. Glasnevin afforded Aylward the opportunity to promote and market education in our Lady of the Angels boarding school as distinctly Irish education for Irish children for the benefit of Irish families.

Schools for the poor and middle classes required teachers trained not only in the art of teaching but also formed in a solid foundation of the teachings of Catholicism. It followed that Miss Aylward had to attend to the recruitment of young women who, ultimately as members of the religious congregation she would establish, would realise her aims for St Brigid's Schools. The boarding school in Glasnevin was to be the linchpin of this strategy. For this work, Aylward had a predilection for young women from rural Ireland. These young women were thought to have 'enthusiasm and buoyancy and mental power and strength of constitution, and withal a simplicity of character'.[15] Glasnevin was an ideal setting for the professional training and spiritual formation of these women of country stock destined for the schools of the Dublin slums.

Just as Glasnevin had been a centre of pilgrimage in the time of Mobhi, it resumed that role for St Brigid's Schools from the time the sisters took up residence. Underpinning religious instruction in the schools was a strong emphasis on Catholic devotions and Catholic sodalities, much of which drew on continental Europe for its inspiration.[16] Instruction in the Catholic faith was no mere rote learning of the catechism. The affective dimension of religious experience was nurtured by a deep and varied devotional life in which processions played an important part, and already in the 1860s and '70s Glasnevin was a centre of pilgrimage for the children of St Brigid's Schools. Miss Aylward was likely heavily influenced by the processions she witnessed while travelling in France.

In 1867, in a letter to Ada Allingham, Aylward described a procession of relics in Aix-la-Chapelle as the 'grandest thing she ever saw'. At one level the letter is an enthusiastic account of a religious experience which the participant found particularly moving. A deeper reading reveals a discourse on the sensory and structural elements of procession and pilgrimage on which many para-liturgical practices relied for the total engagement of their participants. The emphasis on sensory appeal over structure may reveal something of personality of the letter-writer, but the structure of processions reinforcing a hierarchical order even within the framework of affective spiritual experience underpins the account. It is interesting that Margaret instructed Ada to keep the notes of the procession lest she forget the details. Surely such a memory aid had a purpose other than nostalgic recall. In promoting processions in Glasnevin, Margaret Aylward, as the foundress of the St Brigid's network of schools, sought to draw on the sense of place and spiritual heritage to provide meaningful religious experiences within an ordered ecclesial framework.

The scene composition of the 1867 letter describing the procession is complex, with many characters: bishops, priests, friars, nuns, altar servers, children and the streets lined with onlookers. But this was no chaotic press of people. Rather was it ordered, advancing serenely and without hurry. A riot of colour assaults the visual imagination: the glittering jewelled mitres of the archbishop and bishops, vestments of 'every imaginable colour', some richly embroidered in gold, other priests in 'magnificent lace ancients & most valuable trimming', choirboys with scarlet caps, more gold in the cord and tassels of the vibrant painting of the Virgin Mary, a banner of enormous proportions and coloured flags flying from every window. The other senses were not neglected in her account. Thuribles threw out the sweet-smelling incense. Hymns were chanted, prayers recited. When the reliquary had reached the cathedral, the *Te Deum* was sung, a brass band played and cannon thundered a salute. The drama of the procession commanded all the senses to the praise of God. This was the exemplar of the procession which Miss Aylward would introduce for the pupils of St Brigid's Schools, and Glasnevin would emulate Aix-la-Chapelle in providing the setting.[17]

The participants in this procession were clerics, members of religious congregations of women and men, altar servers and children. Adult laypeople were spectators; some joined the procession in prayer as it passed, undoubtedly, but the para-liturgical procession mirrored the Eucharistic liturgy of the period where clerics officiated and the adult laity looked on. It is to be noted that children, on the other hand, participated in the procession, even those who were not altar servers and therefore involved in the liturgy. Was this because they represented innocence or symbolised the works of charity to which many religious orders were committed, or in the hope that they might in the future join the ranks of the clerics? Whatever the reason or reasons, the role of children in processions was guarded and preserved in the Western Church and practised in the procession involving

St Brigid's schoolchildren. The structural elements of the procession are not overstated in the letter but are easily discernible. These elements are most visible in the sequence of order in the procession: the archbishop at the head followed by those who share in the order of bishops; then come the priests, followed by attending altar servers. These liturgical figures are followed by the members of religious orders and the children. Thus is clearly depicted the hierarchical order of the People of God. In a far more modest way such was the experience and ecclesial framework of the processions organised in Glasnevin for the children of St Brigid's Schools, as may be seen in this description of the procession of students from Crow Street which took place on the feast of St James, 25 July 1869:

> The procession set out from the chapel … by St. Kevin's walk … stopped at the cave of Manresa where there was a statue of the Blessed Virgin beautifully decorated with vases of flowers and lighted candles … received a short instruction from Father Gowan … proceeded to St. Joseph's Chapel where Father Gowan spoke again and recited some prayers in which they all joined with the sisters after which they returned to the Chapel where they received Benediction.

The particular role of the children in the procession is described:

> During the procession the Sisters and the Children sang alternately the *Litany of the Blessed Virgin* and some other hymns. In front of the procession was carried a statue of the Blessed Virgin and between each division of the children one of the Sisters carried a banner. After Benediction they went to the school of the convent where they prepared themselves and went home in order.[18]

Another procession in honour of our Lady and St Joseph was held on the Sunday within the Octave of the Assumption, a feast which falls on 15 August. For one such procession in 1877 the children marched 'dressed in white, following the image of our Lady, with their many banners, chanting their litanies and hymns'.[19]

The religious experience of the procession was more than a transitory episode or fleeting encounter; it was to have a lasting effect. Perhaps somewhat surprisingly for a nineteenth-century spirituality permeated by Jansenism, it was intended to be an enjoyable experience for the participants! In contrast to the dour slum environment of inner-city Dublin, the excursion to Glasnevin was indeed an experience of a different place. In Margaret Aylward's view, its memory would sustain the children when, in later life, care and worry beset them: 'This vision of early enjoyment, interwoven with religion, will light up the soul with a ray of hope, and enable her to recover true peace and happiness, which are found only in friendship with God.' The aids to such recollection were entirely sensory, evoking the place of Glasnevin at its best: 'The glorious sunshine; the great wide-spreading green trees; the shady walks; the flowers; the grand procession; the consecration of themselves to the service of God, made on that day, under the protection of our Lady and St. Joseph.'[20]

The procession in Glasnevin replicated the essential sensory and structural elements the procession of relics at Aix-la-Chapelle, albeit in a far more modest and sober fashion. Coupled with the school-based sodalities, the processions made St Brigid's Schools significant contributors to the pastoral strategy of Margaret

Aylward and Cardinal Cullen in the last decade of Cullen's episcopacy and in the religious legacy of both to the city of Dublin.

4

Convent Chapel: Construction, Liturgical Furniture and Decoration

CONSTRUCTION OF CHAPEL

The foundation stone for the new convent chapel was laid in 1898 by Fr Maher CM, who had been appointed by Archbishop Walsh, the Archbishop of Dublin, to take up Fr Gowan's role following his death in the previous year. While the first Mass was celebrated in the chapel on Christmas Day 1899, it was well into the following year before the solemn blessing of the chapel took place. On Pentecost Monday 1900, the sisters from Glasnevin and the other houses, along with the boarders, processed to the chapel for the blessing and Missa Cantata, at which Monsignor Fitzpatrick officiated.

The chapel was dedicated to Our Lady of the Rosary. Perhaps this dedication had been influenced by Fr John Gowan, who had a great devotion to the Blessed Virgin Mary and a strong belief in the efficacy of the rosary. On Easter Sunday 1901, almost a year after the official blessing, the first profession ceremony took place in the chapel when nine sisters made their first profession of vows: Virgilius Walsh, Damien Kennedy, Casimir McDonald, Celsus Raftice, Francis O'Brien, Charles Kennedy, Alphonsus Garen, Columba O'Keefe and Eustochia Carroll. The benefit to the sisters of having a larger and purpose-built chapel is clear, but the study of the chapel building, its fittings and decoration provides an insight into the community of architects, builders and craftsmen active in Dublin at the turn of the century whose skill contributed to this fine neo-Gothic, small, but well – proportioned, chapel.[1]

The well-known Dublin architect William Henry Byrne (1844–1917) was commissioned to design the new chapel. Byrne had earlier worked on the Holy Faith Convent and School in Little Strand Street (1890) and the convent at 115 The Coombe (1895), and was the architect for the reconstruction of the South City Markets in Dublin. He was entrusted with the renovation and interior decoration of St Nicholas of Myra church in Francis Street and the Carmelite church in Clarendon Street, and was also the architect for the new Church of the Assumption in Howth, County Dublin. Outside Dublin he was known for his work in the dioceses of Killala, Tuam and Achonry, in the west of Ireland, and for the diocese of Ossory in the south-east.[2] Much sought after as the architect for Catholic churches, presbyteries and convents, at the time of undertaking the commission for the chapel in Glasnevin Byrne was involved in designing eleven new ecclesiastical buildings and in renovating and extending several others. His plans for the Glasnevin chapel are extant, as are the plans for the slightly later Carmelite church in Blackrock.[3] The similarities between the two plans, along with those of a number of churches and chapels being designed at the same time by Byrne and his assistants, suggest that the architect worked from a basic schema which was modified according to client wishes, available finance and site-specific technical issues.

Three separate sheets constitute the Glasnevin dossier held in the Irish Architectural Archive. Each sheet is headed 'Convent of the Holy Faith Glasnevin, proposed new chapel'. Sheet one shows the floor plan. Sheets two and three, on each of which there is more than one drawing, show the side elevations, east elevation, a longitudinal section, interior of choir and organ gallery, and the sacristies. Written in hand on each sheet are the words 'referred to in agreement dated this 20th day of July 1898, James Kiernan, witness W.S. Clayton'. The only difference between the plans and the building which was eventually realised was the relocation of the sisters' sacristy away from its first position abutting the priests' sacristy to the other side of the chapel, adjacent to Our Lady's side altar. Byrne was paid £50 in 1899 and £76 15s in July 1900.

The contractor for the new chapel was James Kiernan, active as a builder in Dublin from the late 1880s and a leading advocate for the establishment of the Master Builders Association. In 1911, the 63-year-old Kiernan was described in the census as master builder, whereas ten years earlier, in the 1901 census, he was described as a building contractor. Kiernan's business premises were in Talbot Street. In 1903, working with the architect C.G. Ashlin, he received the prestigious commission as contractor for what was the highest building in Dublin at the time, the tower of St Peter's Church, Phibsboro, along with the new nave and aisles.[4] Like W.H. Byrne, Kiernan worked on several building projects for the Holy Faith sisters. In addition to the Glasnevin chapel, and at about the same time, 1900–01, he carried out works on Clarendon Street. In February 1901, he was paid £1,000 for attending to the sewerage in Glasnevin. April of the same year found him building a new 'shed' in Glasnevin for £1,063 16s 1d.[5] Payments to Kiernan for the convent chapel were made in three instalments: £400 in January 1900; £700 in July 1900; and £212 7s 9d in August 1900.

LITURGICAL FURNITURE
AND DECORATION

A feature of the fitting out of the new chapel was the high calibre of craftsmen selected for the fabrication of the liturgical furniture, objects of sacred art and chapel decoration. The highly regarded Edmund Sharp was commissioned to execute the high altar and statue of the Sacred Heart. In 1873 Sharp had arrived in Dublin from his native England, where he had been apprenticed to his brother. In Dublin he worked for Patrick O'Neill and James Pearse, then in partnership. On the dissolution of their partnership, Sharp worked for Pearse, first as foreman and then for ten years, 1877 to 1887, as partner in the firm. He struck out on his own in 1888, establishing a very successful business from his premises in Great Brunswick (later Pearse) Street.

His success was due in large part to his willingness to employ modern technology, such as Rosse's machine which produced carvings of figures and foliage in a far shorter time than that allowed by the conventional hand method. But, unlike some of his competitors Sharp was able to maintain a consistent high quality of workmanship even with the use of modern time-saving methods. By the turn of the century his workshop could turn out one altar per week. Another cost-saving measure was the use of coal gas to drive the machines in his workshop. Coal or town gas was manufactured on his premises at 500 times less than the cost of Dublin town gas. It was not unknown at this time for large industrial firms and institutions to have their own gasworks.[6]

A 1904 photograph in the *Irish Builder* depicting a seated Sharp accompanies an article marking the completion of his altar for the Highgate Chapel, London, designed by the Dublin architects Doolin, Butler and Donnelly.[7] Sharp was not shy of self-promotion; he published a substantial pamphlet listing his major works along with a few pages of favourable press reports on his work. Among religious congregations his largest clients were the Sisters of Mercy, for whom he executed thirty altars, twenty-nine in Ireland and one in Brisbane, capital of the state of Queensland in Australia. The Sisters of Charity had commissioned five altars and, under the heading 'Other', appears Holy Faith Convent, Glasnevin. Sharp elaborated on this commission in his more extensive list of principal works in the same pamphlet, referring to the high altar, fashioned completely from marble, and the statue of the Sacred Heart at Holy Faith Convent, Glasnevin. In this pamphlet he advertised his high altars at a minimum cost of £90.[8]

In addition to his use of modern machinery, Sharp's success was due to his ability to build up a cadre of very able craftsmen. Patrick Tomlin and later his nephew Charles Tomlin were principal sculptors in Sharp's workshop. Tomlin senior was the head sculptor at the time of the commissioning of the Glasnevin altar; he went on to set up his own workshop in Grantham Street.[9]

That Sharp took pride in his workmanship, and that of the sculptors he employed, is evident from his spirited defence in 1903 of the skill of craftsmen associated with church buildings in Ireland and of the aesthetic sense of the Irish clergy, although the latter defence may have been partially influenced by the desire to secure future commissions.[10] The quality of output from Sharp's workshop was evoked in the controversy surrounding the involvement of foreign-born craftsmen in Irish building, a controversy which was not confined to foreign artisans operating in the Irish market but included imported works, particularly those from workshops in Italy. Although always a determined defender of the skill of Irish-born craftsmen, it was a custom of Sharp's to visit the continent at least once a year to inspect new trends in design and technology.

His business continued to expand. His reputation lived on and such was his stature that when he died in a nursing home in 1930, his obituary noted that the sculptor's death 'severs another of the few remaining links with the great period of the Gothic revival'.[11]

The table of Sharp's high altar is still in use in the convent chapel, but the backing altarpiece was removed following renovations to the sanctuary, in line with the liturgical reforms of the Second Vatican Council. In January 1900 Sharp was paid £48 as the balance on the high altar. This sum was donated by Mr James Kavanagh and Messrs Daniel Tallon, Andrew Keogh, and James O'Brien.

Kavanagh had two sisters in the Glasnevin community and owned shops in Wentworth Place and Parliament Street. One of his sisters lived to the age of eighty-three but the other, Brendan, died in May 1904 after a short but painful illness described as 'inward cancer'. Tallon, a widower and wine merchant, had been the Lord Mayor of Dublin 1898–1900. The 1901 census shows him living at 137 Leinster Road with his daughter, niece and a servant. Keogh was an alderman of Dublin City Council. All four donors are described as friends of the congregation by Agnes Vickers, superior of the Glasnevin community when the chapel was being constructed.[12] Sharp's statue of the Sacred Heart is still *in situ* over the Sacred Heart altar in the chapel and is acclaimed for its delicate design and very fine drapery. It was donated by the father of Antoninus Quinn, who had entered the congregation in 1893. Antoninus had another distinction: she was in the last group to be received into the congregation by Fr John Gowan CM, co-founder of the Sisters of the Holy Faith. Uniquely among Holy Faith sisters, she had been born in Douglas on the Isle of Man.

Thos Ryan & Co. supplied the side altars of Our Lady and the Sacred Heart. A well-established company, Ryan had been contracted for the high altar, pulpit and baptismal font for the parish of Clones in the diocese of Clogher, in County Fermanagh. For the side altars of Our Lady and the Sacred Heart in Glasnevin, Ryan was paid £170 with a £5 bonus.[13] The Sacred Heart altar was donated by Mrs O'Farrelly, mother of Sr Athanasius O'Farrelly. An early photograph in the Glasnevin archives shows an altar that is not identical to the marble side altar which is in the chapel in 2013. It is smaller, appears to be manufactured from timber rather than marble, and is painted white with gilded initials on the front panel.[14] It may be concluded that the marble altar was not ready in time, or had not been commissioned, and the timber altar was used until such time as the marble altar became available. This conclusion is supported by the sequence of payments to Thos Ryan & Co. and to Mr Casciani, the artist who gilded the timber altar. The payments to Ryan were in August and

October 1901, and March 1902, whereas the payment to Casciani is dated February 1900, more than a year earlier than the first payment to Ryan. Thus the chapel opened with the temporary gilded altar in place and, at a later date, the marble altar made by Thos Ryan & Co. was installed. The convent account book shows that Antonio Casciani had been responsible for gilding the altar and two branches of candles. For this work he was paid £5 12s 0d and he donated £1 for the erection of the Stations of the Cross which represented a not inconsiderable portion of his earnings, especially for a 30-year-old artist with three young children. Casciani also undertook other tasks, such as lettering the crosses in the cemetery and repairing a pedestal.[15]

It is likely that the workshop of Patrick Beakey supplied the frames for the French-painted Stations of the Cross. Described in 1853 as cabinetmaker to Her Majesty's Board of Works, Beakey was active from at least 1825 with an expanding business in Stafford Street, where he occupied several premises in succession. His major commissions were for the cathedrals of Cobh and Armagh.[16] Although Beakey died in 1867, his workshop continued operating until 1907 and possibly later. The Glasnevin convent account book shows payment in April 1900 to Mr Patrick Beakey, Messrs Cummins & Sons, suggesting that Beakey's business enterprise was operated through the latter's offices. However, the payment is listed 'for the stations' and does not specify the Glasnevin chapel or any other place. Beakey did other work for the congregation, supplying school desks for Clontarf and Clarendon Street.[17] However, the payment for the Stations in the same years as the new chapel was being fitted out strongly suggests that he was the framer of the Stations of the Cross for the convent chapel in Glasnevin.

The fourteen Stations of the Cross themselves remain something of a mystery. The artwork appears to be of a type of ecclesiastical art mass-produced in France in the very late nineteenth century. While the brushwork is unsophisticated, the scene composition is skilful enough. There is one curious feature of the Stations; the title of each Station is painted in French on a near-black band beneath each of the fourteen paintings depicting a stage of the Passion of Jesus. Close examination reveals that these titles are additions. The original text is discernible above the dark band and has been painted over. The original text is in smaller, squarer lettering, whereas the added text is larger and italicised, lending a certain elegance and suggesting a date older than that suggested by the appearance of the original text. On the back of the canvas is stamped 'M. Daniel, Paris, Place St Sulpice'.

In March 1915 the *Irish Builder* reported that 'new decorative panelling has been erected at the community chapel in Glasnevin for the Sisters of the Holy Faith by Mr Kevin Toole from designs prepared by Mr P.J. Munden'.[18] Kevin Toole was a nephew of Richard Toole, who built the Mater Hospital and St Patrick's Drumcondra. Munden was an architect and engineer. He had worked for a while for W.H. Byrne, architect of the convent chapel, before setting up on his own in 1913. In that year he designed an addition to the Clarendon Street school comprising a frontage of 425ft that rose to four storeys. This was the beginning of a long and fruitful association between Patrick Munden and the

Holy Faith congregation, which lasted from 1913 until Munden's death in 1962. Introduced to the Holy Faith sisters by the president of Holy Cross Seminary, Fr Patrick Dunne, Munden worked on so many Holy Faith schools and convents that he was dubbed the architectural advisor for the Holy Faith sisters.[19]

In 1922 the Clarendon Street school was extended when a new three-storey building was added, with a reinforced roof covered with vulcanite which could be used as a roof playground. A similar roof playground was a feature of the extension of Dominick Street. Brennan & Sons of North Strand were the contractors for the 1922 Clarendon Street and the Dominick Street extensions.[20] Munden's major work for the congregation was the design of the new secondary school in Glasnevin, which was completed in 1941. At the time of writing, it continues to operate as St Mary's Secondary School. Its construction is from stock brickwork with buff brick dressings.

Munden also designed all or parts of Haddington Road and Clontarf Schools along with the very fine oratory for Holy Faith Convent, Killester. His last project for Holy Faith was again at Glasnevin, for new classrooms in 1958. Patrick died in 1962. His son, D.J. Munden, had previously joined the company. Mercedes Munden, the architect's daughter, attended the Holy Faith school in Haddington Road before herself becoming an architect and marrying a fellow architect, Frank Purcell, in December 1939. Purcell joined Munden's company, which then traded as Munden & Purcell. Mercedes was an active member of the Holy Faith Past Pupil's Union, attending the annual dance in the Gresham Hotel, patronised by a distinguished past pupil, Senator Miss Margaret Pearse (1878–1968), who was educated at Holy Faith Convent Glasnevin.[21]

Many visitors to the chapel have admired the exquisitely carved seats and prie-dieu. The name of the craftsman was not recorded, but the granddaughter of the wood carver visited Glasnevin convent one day in October 2006 and explained that it was her grandfather, Frederick Phillips of St Joseph's Place, off Upper Dorset Street, who was the mystery carver. Both the 1901 and 1911 censuses record a Frederick Phillips living with his family at 50 St Joseph's Place who stated his occupation as wood carver. The 1901 census gives his birthplace as England, while on the 1911 census form the word Northhampton seems to be written across the columns on either side of the column for birthplace. Phillip's granddaughter stated that Frederick worked in the convent for many years and was paid every Friday by Sr Appollonia Cassidy, who always sent home some food and treats for the family, which in 1901 numbered four children and by 1911 had grown to six. At that time Appollonia Cassidy had charge of the convent accounts and it would have fallen to her to make these regular payments.

The renowned French-trained organ builder John White built the one-manual organ in the convent chapel. White built the original organs for the St Mary's Pro-Cathedral in Marlborough Street, Dublin, and the Jesuit church in Gardiner Street, Dublin. Though each has been extensively renovated, some of White's original pipes remain. Paul McKeever has shown that White not only used French reeds, but flue pipework characteristic of the work of arguably the most influential organ builder of the nineteenth century, Aristide Cavaillé-Coll.[22] An advertisement for White's organs concluded: 'all latest improvements, combining simplicity of mechanism, silent, easy action and durability-qualities seldom found in organs generally. Two hundred are erected in various Catholic churches'.[23] White was paid £150 for the Glasnevin organ in November 1901. A Mr Theodore Logier was employed to give organ lessons to the sisters. Theodore and his father, John, were music teachers and performers of some repute. At the time of his employment as organ tutor in Glasnevin convent, Theodore Logier would have been 28 years old.

STAINED-GLASS WINDOWS

The stained-glass windows in the apse of the chapel were manufactured by Mayer & Co., who supplied stained glass for many ecclesiastical buildings in Ireland up to and beyond the establishment of An Túr Gloine. In Dublin, the Augustinian church in John's Lane boasts impressive examples of Mayer's work: the five windows of the apse and the Great Window over the entrance. The Heritage Council chose a Mayer window as the cover of its book on the conservation of stained glass.[24]

A family-run Munich-based company, still in operation, Mayer was founded in 1847 to foster the traditions of medieval art and architecture, particularly in the production of stained glass. In response to great demand, branches were set up in London in 1865 and New York in 1888.[25] Joshua Clarke, father of Harry

Clarke, was Mayer's agent in Ireland, in addition to operating his own church decorating and stained-glass business from North Frederick Street. After Joshua died in 1921, the business was managed by his sons, Harry and Walter.[26]

For the Glasnevin chapel Mayer supplied the small Holy Family rose window in 1900 at a cost of £30, donated by Mr John O'Brien, and the small nativity rose window in 1901, also at a cost of £30. The cost of the remaining stained-glass windows, the locations of which are not specified, amounted to a sum of £120, paid on 17 July 1900. A plaque records the names of the donors in Latin: James Kavanagh, Daniel Tallon, Andrew Keogh, and John O'Brien. It appears that between them these four men paid for all the stained-glass windows in the sanctuary, as the plaque commemorating their donation uses the plural 'these windows' (*hac fenestras*). It is not possible to know from the placement of the plaque whether or not their gift included the plain coloured-glass windows of the nave and transept, but based on the sum paid, £120, it is more likely that it included only the trio of windows behind the high altar, and that the aisle and transept windows were paid for from other sources. A slightly later installation date for the aisle and transept windows is also suggested by the identical design with the windows in the gable end of the second generation school, now the old school hall of St Mary's Secondary School.

A study of Mayer's output and style notes that 'stylistically, Mayer's windows tend to contain richly coloured scenes bordered by architectural frames consisting of pilasters, columns, architraves and elaborate canopies'.[27] These architectural elements are to be found in some windows designed by Mayer for Holy Faith convents but are absent in the Mayer windows of Glasnevin chapel. The English artist William Francis Dixon joined Mayer & Son in 1894. His 'bewitching work' heralds touches of Harry Clarke, particularly in the treatment of facial features. Dixon's style is characterised by 'sweetness of drawing, softness of painting and beautiful tapestry-like details', but the chapel windows lack this level of sophistication and artistry.[28] Thus it is reasonable to conclude that the chapel windows come from Mayer's stock of lower-priced ecclesiastical art.

Three windows adorn the sanctuary wall behind the high altar. The Virgin Mary is depicted in the centre window, with St Brigid and St Patrick in the windows either side. The iconography is traditional but features elements characteristic of Mayer's approach to the iconography of the Madonna, angels and saints. In the centre, the deep-blue mantle of the Virgin has a highly decorative border with a narrow band of beads separating the border from the main sweep of the mantle. The border itself is decorated in lighter blue with six-pointed stars of medium and larger size. Stars feature in Mayer's treatment of the Virgin to reference her title of Queen of Heaven. The tunic, both torso and sleeves, is similarly decorated with six-pointed stars in the same cream or ivory colour as the tunic. The Virgin holds a sceptre in her left hand and in her right hand presents the Child with full face forward, holding in his hand a pair of rosary beads. The lower panel of the window bears the words in Latin, 'Our Lady of the Rosary, pray for us'. The inclusion of the rosary honours the dedication of the chapel under the title of Our Lady of the Rosary.

The treatment of St Patrick is conventional, with the figure depicted in green and carrying a staff around which some serpents are coiled. The design of the cope is similar to that of the Virgin's mantle with a narrow band of beads demarcating the border, which, in a lighter green tone, is adorned with alternating liturgical and episcopal symbols. The lower panel of the window bears the words in Latin 'one Lord, one faith, St Patrick, pray for us'.

St Brigid completes the trio. She is depicted as a sombre figure, clad in plum-coloured robes with a lighter shade for the inner robe. Her figure and robes are totally devoid of decoration. In symmetry with the figure of St Patrick, the lower panel of St Brigid's window bears the words in Latin 'one Lord, one faith, St Brigid, pray for us'.[29] Oral tradition in the congregation has it that this trio of windows was removed in the early 1940s to repair the glazing bars and that when they were reinstated the light had lost some of its lustre.

THE 1901 CENSUS: VILLAGE AND CONVENT COMMUNITY

1901

The census of 1901 provides a snapshot of the convent
community in Glasnevin at the start of the twentieth
century. However, analysis of the census is limited in its
depth. It cannot tell us anything about the morale, mood,
degree of cohesion and unity of spirit in the community.
The decade following the 1901 census, especially the years
1910–11, was a time of some turbulence in the internal
organisation of the congregation, and some of the main
actors lived in the Glasnevin community. However, by its
very nature, the census information provides only the
barest background to the events of the years that followed.

Before the census was taken in March 1901, Queen
Victoria died. She had visited Dublin in the spring of
the previous year and had been observed in a carriage
enjoying a drive around Glasnevin![1] In 1901, Marconi –
connected to Jameson's Distilleries through his mother,
Anne Jameson – sent his first wireless transmission;
the first Nobel Prizes were awarded; Australia became
a federation; Kodak introduced the Brownie camera.
In Ireland a national consciousness was germinating.
The Gaelic Athletic Association, the Gaelic League –
whose aim was to promote the Irish language – and the
Irish National Theatre Society (later the Abbey) had all
been founded in the embers of the previous century.
Dubliners moved into the new century completely
unaware of the conflicts, both domestic and worldwide,
which lay before them.

The year 1901 was a watershed for Glasnevin village.
In that year Glasnevin, formerly a township along
with Drumcondra and Clonliffe, was incorporated

into the city of Dublin under the control of the Dublin
Corporation, now the Dublin City Council. First proposed
in 1877, the integration of the township encountered
severe opposition from the long-established residents of
Glasnevin, who were intent on preserving the pastoral
character of the area.[2] The proponents of integration
enjoyed the support of Cardinal Cullen, while Henry Gore
Lindsay was one of the leading opponents of the proposal.
An immediate outcome of the Corporation's takeover was
the attention paid to water supply and sewerage for the
suburbs. This probably explains the convent's expenditure
of the very large sum of £1,000 in 1901 for sewerage works
on the convent site. Residual opposition to development
meant that it was not until after the First World War that
new housing began to appear north of the Tolka. At this
time, the master builder, Alexander Strain, began to build
substantial homes in Glasnevin, having earlier been active
in Drumcondra, Iona and Lindsay Roads, and other
areas of Glasnevin south of the Tolka.[3] On the cusp of
enormous social and political change in Ireland and
abroad, and stirrings in the local area, the national census
was taken on the night of Sunday 31 March 1901.

GLASNEVIN VILLAGE
AT THE TIME OF THE CENSUS

By 1901, some of the familiar names and personalities
in Glasnevin had disappeared. The Holy Faith
community's most immediate neighbours were the
inhabitants of Roseville, directly across the road from
the entrance to the convent. As depicted in Brendan

Scally's sketch, Roseville was a neat, two-storey Georgian dwelling. It was owned by the Lindsay family, who lived in it for a few years in the early nineteenth century but for the most part used it a residence for visiting guests such as Viscount Ikerrin, who had married into the Lindsay family.[4] His family, the Butlers, had been raised to the Irish peerage as Viscounts Ikerrin and Earls of Carrick in 1629. In the English peerage they were the Barons of Mount Juliet, County Kilkenny.

The Butlers were related to the Lindsays through the marriage of Henry Gore Lindsay's eldest daughter Ellen Rosamund to Charles Butler, 7th Earl of Carrick. The marriage took place in St Mobhi's church, Glasnevin, in November 1898. Their first son, Theobald Walter Butler, later 8th Earl of Carrick, was born in May 1903, but he does not appear in the baptismal records of St Mobhi's for that year. From 1946 the site was occupied by the Institute of Industrial Research & Standards, in a building designed by Buckley and O'Gorman with J. Brennan & Sons, North Strand, as the contractor. An extension was completed in 1958.[5] Between its construction and 2010, the building was known by several equally uninspiring names: Eolas, Irish Science and Technology, Enterprise Ireland and Forbairt. The site was occupied in 2013 by Dublin City University.

On Glasnevin Hill, or Washerwoman's Hill, to give it its much used but unofficial name, quite the most interesting house is Beechmont. First occupied by a Huguenot family named Batho, in 1901 it was in the ownership of Andrew Ryan, publican, but was occupied by his brother Timothy, his servant and two boarders. Andrew lived at 20 Church Road with his wife and one servant.

Beechmount has been handsomely restored and stands slightly recessed from the road. In the 1901 census it was listed as house No. 2. No. 1 was occupied by the Parnells, a Methodist family with five children. William, the father, was a head gardener possibly for the nearby Botanic Gardens. The Delanys' old house, Delville, was occupied by the barrister Stephen Lanigan-O'Keefe, with this wife, four sons and two daughters, and four female domestic servants. The entire household was Catholic.[6] Born in Tipperary, Stephen was the son of John Lanigan, barrister and Member of Parliament, and he added his mother's maiden name of O'Keefe to Lanigan in 1895.[7] The family retained ownership of the house until 1932. Eventually it became the Bons Secours Hospital.

The Catholic Church of Our Lady of Dolours occupies a pretty but flood-prone position beside the bridge of the village. The present church, with its distinctive pyramid roof, replaced the former wooden structure, 'The Woodener'. In 1901 Glasnevin belonged to the parish of Fairview; it was not constituted as a parish in its own right until 1912.

Almost directly across the road was Tolka House. Known earlier as 'The Bull's Head', it existed at least from the beginning of the eighteenth century.[8] Then came the row of houses known as St Vincent's Terrace, which seemed to teeter on the steep incline of the hill until their demolition in the 1970s. The corner house was a well-preserved two-storey Georgian dwelling, with five windows on the second storey, the panes arranged in four over four pattern. The old forge was adjacent to the convent site and is now a restaurant.

Historically by far the most significant building in Glasnevin is St Mobhi's church. The present building dates from 1707 and is the result of an appeal from the parishioners to Archbishop King to rebuild the centuries-old church, which had fallen into ruins. Sir John Rogerson headed the group making the appeal and was one of the chief subscribers to the public subscription for the new building. Extensions were added in 1896 and again in 1908, with major restoration works in 1962.

Perhaps of equal, if not greater, significance, is the churchyard cemetery.[9] Buried there is Patrick Delany of Delville with his first wife, Margaret Tennison, and, in the neighbouring plot, the Lindsay family – except for Bishop Charles Lindsay who is entombed in Christ Church Cathedral. The Craigies of Merville dairy are there, along with Thomas Tickell of the Botanic Gardens and many of the landowners in Glasnevin and its vicinity.

Equally as fascinating as the iconic buildings of Glasnevin and their inhabitants is the census data on the occupants of the dwellings, which shows an emerging diversity in the population of Glasnevin. Although the division between the old Church of Ireland families and the Catholic poor, who were generally servants or labourers, remained dominant, new groups of upwardly mobile Catholics and Protestants appear. The Lindsay family was still in Glasnevin, living just up the road from the convent at 23 Church Hill, Naul Road (now Ballymun Road).[10] Henry Gore Lindsay, aged 70, was in residence with his wife, Ellen Sarah, aged 64. There were no adult children living with them. Six servants made up the remainder of the household. The Lindsay family, housekeeper, footman and groom were members of the Church of Ireland, whereas the kitchen maid, the housemaid and a servant were Catholics.

However, of the twenty-one households before the Lindsay's house, ten were populated by Church of Ireland families and seven by Catholics. The remaining three were populated by Baptist, Presbyterian, and Plymouth Brethren families. Six of the Church of Ireland families had one or more servants. In all cases the servants were Catholics. The occupations listed for the Church of Ireland families were tea buyer, architect, dairy proprietor, magistrate, tea and wine merchant, solicitor, and clerk in the GPO. Occupations listed for the Catholics were labourer, medical student, gardeners, a customs and excise officer, and a jeweller. The father in the Baptist family was a commercial traveller and the Plymouth Brethren man was a draughtsman in the Registry of Titles. The presence of a medical student, customs officer and a jeweller amongst the Catholic population shows a shift away from servant and labouring classes as well as a level of equality with the Protestant groups. In Dublin there had been gradual increase in the representation of Catholics in the middle-class occupations. In law and medicine the rise was spectacular. Alongside its more Catholic neighbouring suburb of Drumcondra, which had gained a reputation for revelry, Glasnevin continued to have a high proportion of Church of Ireland adherents.[11]

Emerging diversity is not evident in the twelve cottages of Church Lane, where all households were Catholic except one, which was Church of Ireland. There were seven general labourers – the most common occupation

recorded for men – and three others who are specifically
listed as a labourer in the Botanic yard, a farm, and a
builder's labourer. Other occupations listed for men
were gardeners and a grocer's porter. Of the two men
recorded as clerks, one was a Catholic and the other an
adherent of the Church of Ireland. Six occupations were
recorded for women: clerk, mantle-maker, dressmaker,
housekeeper, laundress and servant.[12] By the time of the
1911 census, dressmaking had become the most popular
occupation for women outside domestic service.

The River Tolka flows through the convent lands in
Glasnevin and forms the boundary with the Botanic
Gardens. Although no industrial activity took place
on this particular stretch of the river, the Tolka was
an important source of water power for the emerging
industrial development of North Dublin in the
nineteenth century. A woollen mill was established near
Mobhi Road using water from a mill race connected
with the flour mill at the junction of Millbourne Avenue
and Upper Drumcondra Road.[13] Local industry in the
immediate vicinity of the convent centred on Craigie's
Dairy on Church Road, where George Craigie's two
eldest sons managed the dairy business with the help of
four dairy yard labourers.

Further evidence of the far-reaching influence of the
Lindsay family in Glasnevin lies in the fact that George
Lindsay was listed as occupier of the house between 1855
and 1877.[14] The elder Craigie son, aged 27, was a cattle
salesman and his brother, younger by one year, was listed
as the proprietor of the dairy. Their father was recorded
as being an architect, but he appears not to have been
very active in his profession. The dairy comprised three

cow houses, one calf house, sundry other sheds and a turf house, bringing the total number of outhouses to twelve, surpassed on the road only by Lindsay, who had fourteen outhouses but none concerned with cattle. The Craigie family moved from Church Road in 1925 and set up the Merville Dairy on Finglas Road. The Wexford Dairy, a Nolan family enterprise, did not begin until 1918, when the Nolans took up residence in Church Road.[15] The house and land, covering a quarter of an acre, was offered for auction in June 2013 with an advertised market value of €250,000. It had been the subject of several planning applications since 2006, all of which were submitted on behalf of Maylock, a company of developers whose registered company office is in Griffith Avenue, Glasnevin.[16]

HOLY FAITH CONVENT COMMUNITY IN 1901 CENSUS

The religious community of Holy Faith sisters in Glasnevin was listed on Form A, which was the basic household return, covering name, age, sex, relationship to head of the household, religion, occupation, marital status, and county or country of birth of every person in the house on the night of the census. Also recorded on this form was an individual's ability to read or write, ability to speak Irish, and whether he or she suffered from any infirmity.

The 1901 census form for Glasnevin convent was signed by Margaret Vickers, who was listed as the superior of the Glasnevin community, but was known in the community as Agnes.[17] A short, rotund woman in middle age, she was appointed the first superior-general in 1899, following the death of the foundress Margaret Aylward, and elected to that office in 1904. She died 31 December 1907, having completing almost four years of her six-year term of office.

In 1901 the community numbered seventy-one sisters whose average age was 30, the oldest being 73 and the youngest 16. The breakdown of ages in ten-year brackets was: one sister in 70s; three in 60s; ten in 50s; six in 40s; eight in 30s, thirty-one in 20s and twelve under 20. The census form listed all sisters as instructors of youth. Whether that was a term chosen by Agnes Vickers or the census enumerator it is impossible to know, yet the term is grounded in the spiritual heritage of the young congregation. Fr Gowan wrote of the sisters that they had but 'one object, one purpose, one work, that is the instruction of youth'.[18] All sisters are listed as unmarried and no infirmities are recorded for any sister. The seventy-one members included individuals in the first three years of trying out their vocation in the congregation as well as those who had made vows for three years and renewed them. Final vows were not made in the congregation until 1904.

Twenty-three of the seventy-one sisters in Glasnevin community were born in Dublin or County Dublin. Nine hailed from Tipperary and an equal number from Kilkenny. Five were born in Kildare, with four from Wicklow and an equal number from Cork, and three from each of Waterford, Westmeath and Kerry. One sister was born on the Isle of Man and another in Lancashire. One came from each of Roscommon, Limerick, Clare, Carlow, Meath and Queen's County (Offaly). Thirty-two of the seventy-one are listed as speaking both Irish and English, including the sister born in Lancashire.

The oldest member of the community in 1901 was Mary Markey, who had entered thirty-seven years earlier in December 1864. She made her first profession of vows on 15 August 1869 but died in 1903, one year before final vows were permitted. The youngest in the 1901 Glasnevin community who remained in religious life was Elizabeth Delany, who was given the name de la Salle. She was a sister to Cronan and Alberta Delany. Having entered the community in 1899, she made her first profession in 1902, renewed her vows in 1905, and died two years later from consumption. Thus it was that neither the oldest nor the youngest community member in Glasnevin in 1901 made final vows.

The fact that so many sisters came from outside Dublin when Holy Faith activity was limited to Dublin, Wicklow and Kildare may be partly explained by Margaret Aylward's determination to attract country girls to the boarding school in pursuit of her desire to encourage them to become teachers and embrace religious life, but another significant factor is associated with the dower. No dower was required of those wishing to enter the Holy Faith congregation, in contrast to many other orders in Ireland at the time. Indeed the Presentation and other congregations frequently referred young woman without a dower to the Holy Faith. Margaret Aylward had a quiet disdain for the trappings of wealth brought to convents by some aspirants. From France she wrote: 'a young lady of this house goes to a Convent next week & such preparations, satin frock, silver handle knife & silver drinking cup gilt inside, with white water silk dress with a bouquet of orange flowers.'[19] For her part, Aylward was convinced that aspirants with a reasonable intellectual capacity were more important to a teaching order than were aspirants with dowers but possessed of limited intellectual prowess. This openness to accepting women from less affluent backgrounds caused difficulty for the congregation with the Holy See, leading to a long delay in the final approval of the constitutions of the Sisters of the Holy Faith.[20]

Even thirty-five years after the arrival of the Holy Faith sisters in Glasnevin, there were some in the 1901 community who had strong links to the early days of the congregation. Margaret Gaughren and Margaret (Agnes) Vickers were two of the first three women to join Margaret Aylward and Ada Allingham. With Mary Ann Vickers they were in the first group to come to Glasnevin in 1865. Links to Fr Gowan, the Vincentian priest recognised as the co-founder of the congregation, were strong. Gonzaga (Gertrude) Landy, who entered in 1877, was his niece and two community members, Germanus (Catherine) Barry and Rosalie (Mary) Craddock, had been received as novices by him. Three of the five signatories to the 1895 letter to Pope Leo XIII asking for papal recognition as a religious congregation were members of the Glasnevin community in 1901: Agnes Vickers who signed as superior; Rose Gaughren who signed as mistress of novices; Apollonia Cassidy who signed as procuratrix general. As might be expected, this cohort of older sisters who had known Margaret Aylward and Fr Gowan were devoted to their memory, their aims and their methods.

Blood relatives were to be found in the Glasnevin community. There were four sets of sisters. The Carrolls, from Westmeath, were twins and aged 52 in 1901.

Entering in May of 1874, but a few weeks apart, were the Walsh sisters, Bride (Rose) and Augustine (Catherine). Bride, aged 52 in 1901, was the elder by four years. Tipperary-born Damian (Honoria) and Charles (Brigid) Kennedy entered in the same year, 1898. The fourth set of sisters in the community was the Reillys from Westmeath: Paul (Agnes) entered in 1898 aged 21 and Emilian (Catherine) was aged 18 on entry. Successive generations of the same family were in the community. Brigid Vickers and her sister, Josephine (Patricia) were the nieces of Agnes Vickers and Mary Ann Vickers. The two Russells were mother and daughter.

In 1901 twenty-seven of the Glasnevin community members spoke Irish. Indicating affirmative in the Irish column could have meant anything from a very limited knowledge of Irish to full fluency. Sr Ligouri Carmody, from Clare, was a native Irish speaker. Neither in 1901 nor 1911 was the teaching of Irish compulsory. Indeed Mr Eamon de Valera, former leader of the Fianna Fáil Party and President of Ireland, recalled how his wife Sinéad, a passionate advocate of the Irish language and fluent speaker of Irish, gave lessons in Irish to the sisters in Greystones, encouraged them to include it in the school curriculum and herself gave lessons to the students in the school in Greystones.[21]

The national census provided a separate form for college and boarding-school returns. This Form G collected information under the same categories as Form A. For the boarding school at Glasnevin seventy-five pupils are recorded, all but four born in Ireland.[22] The majority, fifty-two, came from Dublin, evidence, perhaps of the waning of the determination to recruit country girls to the school. Of the remainder, two came from Antrim, the only representatives from what was to become Northern Ireland. From the counties of Leinster came five from County Kildare, two from each of Counties Wicklow, Louth and Meath, and one from County Offaly. Munster contributed two from County Tipperary, and one from each of counties Cork, Limerick, Waterford, and Kerry. Monaghan and Roscommon provided one each and one pupil had no place of birth recorded against her name. Two sisters surnamed Savage had been born in 'America', one surnamed Clinton was born in Australia and another surnamed Shepherd was born in India.

Since 1892, attendance at school had been compulsory for children aged 6 to 14. The age breakdown of the pupils was: fourteen under 10 years of age, with six of the fourteen under 6 years of age; twenty-eight between 10 and 13; twenty-six between 14 and 16; six between 17 and 19, and three aged 20 or over. All fourteen pupils aged 10 and under, with one exception, were from Dublin. The exception was the one pupil from America.

Only five pupils are listed as having Irish; confirmation that Irish was not part of the curriculum in 1901. Of the five who had Irish, all were aged 15 or over. Two came from Tipperary, one from Kerry, another from Limerick and the fifth was from County Dublin. Age and county of origin suggest that the students had acquired their knowledge of Irish in the primary schools of their respective counties or in their homes.

The custom of having lay sisters – that is to say, a clearly defined group of sisters whose principal duty was to cook, clean and in some cases wait on the

community sisters – was never a feature of Holy Faith
life. In some congregations, even congregations of
apostolic life, such lay sisters were distinguished from the
other sisters in dress, in taking their meals at a different
time, or in a different dining room, and having official
recreation periods separate from the other sisters. When
in France, Margaret Aylward had taken particular note
of a religious congregation which did not distinguish
between choir and lay sisters but had only one 'class'
among them: 'I forgot to say the Franciscan Sisters have
only sisters, all are the same class.'[23] A small number of
sisters indicated on entering the Holy Faith congregation
that they would be happy to be cooks or assist in the
domestic life of the community, but all sisters took turns
in cleaning and other domestic duties.[24] This is borne out
in the convent financial records. In 1900 the payments
designated wages in the cash books are recorded as wages
for farm workers. No payments are recorded for cooking
and cleaning services performed by employees for the
sisters. Some sisters were engaged in various services for
the community including ordering provisions, keeping
the financial accounts, looking after the sick, cooking,
cleaning, sewing, supervising the farm, and taking the
role of sacristan – that is having the care of everything to
do with the chapel and the services that took place in it.
Sr Alexis Nugent served as the sacristan in Glasnevin for
thirty-nine years from 1901, but she was not present on
the night of the census.

It is tempting to look to this community of women for
insight into the role of women as managers of households
in late nineteenth- and early twentieth-century Dublin.
Such an inquiry has recently been undertaken in respect

of elite women in nineteenth-century Ireland, but the
women in the Glasnevin convent community were far
from the class of socially elite, as a study of those who
brought dowers with them shows.[25] Only twenty-three
of the seventy-one community members in 1901 had
brought a dower at the time of their entry. Of these
twenty-three sisters only four had dowers in excess of
£100, the highest being £300. Eight dowers were under
£50 and eleven between £100 and £150.[26]

On the evidence of the dowers alone, the social and
financial status of the community members was anything
but elite. Moreover, the hierarchical structure of religious
community life, along with the unofficial and hidden
power relations within it, make it extremely difficult to
identify the decision-makers in the management and
provision of the household. O'Riordan has shown
that on the estates of the landed gentry the dairy and
farm came under the care of the landowner's wife.[27]
The Vickers sisters, neither of whom brought a dowry,
ran the farm, and in 1901 Agnes was the superior of the
community. Without doubt Agnes Vickers was an able
enough woman, but her ability in farm management did
not stem from a privileged background but possibly from
her family background in rural County Dublin.

SUPPLIERS TO CONVENT COMMUNITY

A more profitable line of inquiry may lie in assessing
the information that may be gleaned from convent
records on expenditure on supplies. This assessment
throws light on the retail, industrial and commercial

activity of the city. Agnes Vickers was recognised as having introduced a dietary regime of a slightly more humane kind; for example, butter to accompany the bread offered at lunch. Rose Gaughren states that up to that time only dry bread was available, which the sisters would soften in thick skimmed milk or hold under the water pipe in school to moisten it! This practice is corroborated in an anonymous and undated account of the early days in the congregation.[28]

Edmund Downes was one of the bread suppliers to Glasnevin. His bakery is featured in James Joyce's *Dubliners*. Maria in *Clay* bought six mixed penny cakes in Downes's when she alighted from the tram at the Pillar. Downes's shop was in North Earl Street. Maria thought the plumcake lacked sufficient almond icing and crossed Sackville Street to the other side of The Pillar to a shop in Henry Street, where she bought plumcake more to her liking before catching the tram to Drumcondra. The sisters in Glasnevin bought bread from Downes' bakery – maybe because it was a well-known enterprise, but also because Downes himself was a neighbour of the sisters in Eccles Street.

Five sisters were living in the convent in 46 Eccles Street in 1901 and Joseph Downes with his wife and four children lived a few doors down at 40 Eccles Street. The Glasnevin community continued to be supplied by Downes for decades to come. Bermingham's supplied meat and Mulligan's was the main suppliers of groceries. Fruit trees were purchased from Watson's. Given that the Glasenvin property had been established for many years, it is likely that there were already mature trees providing some fruit. Occasionally oranges were purchased.

The most expensive non-food maintenance item was the repair of boots! This is consistent with the wear and tear on boots which would be the result of so many sisters walking from Glasnevin to teach in the city schools each day. Tram travel was an occasional means of transport. Books of tickets were bought monthly for £3 15s, perhaps for travel to school in inclement weather.

Gas was supplied by the Alliance and Dublin Consumer's Gas Company. With headquarters in D'Olier Street, its main works were at Sir John Rogerson's quay.[29] T.&C. Martin, from whom the timber for the stage in the hall was obtained, was a large-scale joinery plant. Opening in 1859 on the North Wall, by 1861 it employed 100 joiners. The eldest daughter in the Martin family of twelve children was Marie, later Mother Mary, Martin who founded the Medical Missionaries of Mary.

Sharkey's foundry supplied the crosses for the sisters' graves for the convent cemetery in Glasnevin. Manhole covers in Church Street bore the name 'Sharkey'. The foundry's position was a strategic location in the Easter Rising of 1916. A company commander was ordered to 'occupy the position from the corner of Hammond Lane to Sharkey's Iron Foundry which commanded Chancery Lane'.[30] On the death of a sister, a pound was given to the 'man who brought the coffin'. In later years, and to this day, the congregation is served by the undertaking firm of Corrigan & Sons, who began operations in 1884 in Camden Street.[31] Christmas boxes were given to the farm workers, the postman and the baker's man.

From the scant available evidence it is impossible to build up a complete picture of the operations of the farm. The Vickers sisters, Agnes and Mary, had charge

of the farm around 1900. Apart from the wages for the
farm workers, regular expenses included the purchase
of grain, oats, bran and manure. Mountjoy brewery,
from which grain was obtained, was founded in Dublin
in 1852 by a Scot, Alexander Findlater. The firm had
extensive export destinations, mainly to those bastions
of empire, Gibraltar, Malta, Cyprus, and to Britain
itself. The North City Milling Company, from which
the convent purchased oats and bran, was once one of
the largest mills in Dublin. Exploiting the proximity of
the Royal Canal to the Midland and Great Western
Railways, its premises on Glasnevin Road manufactured
mainly oatmeal, Indian meal and flour. Its proximity
to Glasnevin was likely to have been one of the reasons
for the convent's purchases of grain from the company.
Founded by the Murtagh brothers, by the end of the
1870s the mill had been overtaken in size by Boland's mill
at Ringsend, but it continued trading and the company
was not dissolved until 1990. The Murtagh brothers were
established as provender millers and grain merchants in
1887 in Middle Abbey Street, before installing themselves
in Blackhall Street and moving to Ashbourne in 2013.[32]
Manure for the convent farm was supplied by Campbell,
McKeon and other unnamed sources.

Additionally, farm machinery such as plough wheels
and carts had to be repaired. James Fitzpatrick carried out
some of these repairs. Horses had to be shod, and the vet,
name unrecorded, was paid one guinea per visit at a time
when the doctor was paid one pound per visit.

Four small dwellings were situated towards the Finglas
end of the site. Given that the male in each dwelling is
listed as labourer, it is highly likely that these men worked

as labourers on the convent farm.[33] One three-roomed house was occupied by the Atley family. Anne Atley, aged 60 and a widow, headed a household of herself, her older widowed sister, her two adult children, and two grandchildren. Her son, Patrick, aged 35, was a labourer and unmarried. Her daughter Catherine, a dressmaker, was aged 28 and unmarried. The grandchildren, Thomas Atley and Annie Mason, were both aged 4 and both attended school. It is not possible to know who the parents of the grandchildren were or if, indeed, the grandchildren lived with Anne or just happened to be staying there on the night of the census. All members of the household were born in County Dublin and all were Roman Catholics. Anne herself could read but not write. Her sister and her adult children could both read and write.

An older couple occupied one of the other houses: John Brennan or Brannen, aged 66, and his wife Bridget, aged 60. Both were born in County Meath. John was a farm labourer and Mary a housekeeper. John could read but not write and Mary could neither read nor write. Both John and Mary were Roman Catholics.

The Collins family occupied another house. They were: Robert, aged 45; his wife Anne, aged 28; and their four children Josephine aged 7, John aged 6, James aged 4, and Anne aged 2. Robert was a labourer; Anne's occupation is not recorded. Both could read and write. All were born in Dublin and were Roman Catholics. The census form shows Catholic spelt with an 'e' at the end of the word.

The occupiers of the last house on the convent property in 1901 were the Flood family: Patrick, born in Dublin, and Eliza, born in County Meath, their three children and a young boarder. At 46, Patrick was younger than his wife by three years. They had two adult unmarried children: John aged 22, a labourer, and Catherine aged 21, a dressmaker. Patrick, a labourer, could not read or write whereas Eliza could read but not write. Both adult children could read and write. A second daughter, Maggie, aged 16, was still at school. The boarder was Cecil Burke, aged 3. His relationship to the Flood family is unknown. In 1911 he was living with his parents in Sandford Road, Rathmines.

Outhouses and farm buildings help to round out the picture of farming activity. The lists of such buildings in the 1901 and 1911 census of the convent throw some light on the farming activities and animals kept. Outhouses and farm buildings registered by the census enumerator are fewer for 1911 than for 1901. In 1901 there were twenty-six out-offices, and in 1911 there were sixteen. Both in 1901 and 1911 there was one each of a dairy, potato house and workhouse. Increasing in number were the buildings for the coachhouse, from two to three, and the laundry from none to two. Halving in number from four to two were the stables and cow houses respectively, and the piggery, fowl houses and turf houses from two to one respectively. Disappearing completely were the calf houses, harness room, sheds and storehouse.

The reduction of buildings indicates a scaling back of farm activity in the ten years between 1901 and 1911. This would be a curious development, especially as we know that the population of sisters and of boarders remained constant. However, given the very large expenditure of a thousand pounds on unspecified 'sheds' in April 1901, after the census was taken, it is possible that some of the outhouses were replaced by new facilities

Aylward House, formerly St Brigid's Primary School.

which, though fewer in number, may have been larger and increased rather than diminished overall capacity.

In the year of the census, building on the site continued. The convent chapel was completed and the building of the second generation St Mary's School, the building next to Aylward House as one approaches the chapel, was being planned. It was built in 1903 and between 1903 and 1941 it accommodated classrooms for day pupils on the ground floor and sleeping accommodation for the boarders on the upper floor. The boarders had lessons in the convent, separately from the day pupils. When the new boarding school was opened in 1941, this practice ceased and boarders and day students were mixed in classes. The building was then used as a private junior school until 1986 when such schools were phased out. In 2013, St John's Educational Centre was located in the building.

6

THE SITE TAKES
ITS PRESENT SHAPE

ST MARY'S SECONDARY SCHOOL

St Mary's Secondary School, still one of the largest single constructions in Glasnevin, enjoys a commanding position above the lands sweeping down to the Tolka, the vista extending across the Botanic Gardens, the skyline punctuated by the cedar of Lebanon in the convent grounds and the O'Connell monument standing in Prospect Cemetery. Its architect, P.J. Munden, presented a first set of drawings which was a stunning design for a Boarding School and Young Ladies Hostel. Two storeys built around two courtyards, with the dining hall separating them, afforded 100 single rooms on the first floor with the necessary amenities and a series of study rooms, classrooms, parlours, cloakrooms, dining and kitchen facilities on the lower floor. The boarding school was to be a mirror image of the hostel. It appears that the hostel function was dropped, and the building which eventuated was not the mirrored half of the original design but an entirely new design in which individual rooms were abandoned in favour of dormitory accommodation.[1]

The contractor, R. Macken of Synge Street, was involved in the huge primary school development in Drimnagh which, at its completion in 1943, had an enrolment of 3,800 pupils, ranking it among the largest school developments in Europe of its time. Macken completed the Glasnevin school in fourteen months. The consulting engineer was M. Matthews, the quantity surveyor T. Kavanagh, the heating engineers Musgrave Ltd, the electrical engineers, Roche and McConnell. The construction of the new school altered the built environment in the grounds. The 'Temple',

which had served as an isolation unit and later fruit store,
along with St Joseph's Grotto on the upper walk, had to
be demolished to make way for the new construction.

Although Mother Regis Phelan was the driving force
behind the building of the new boarding school, she died
before the foundation stone was laid and her successor,
Mother Elizabeth Kelly, led the congregational representation at the ceremony on 8 December 1939 when
Monsignor Walsh, PP Glasthule, blessed the foundation
stone to great acclaim and a who's who attendance of
political and judicial figures.

Many years later, Dorothy Munden, the architect's
daughter-in-law, found a document which she returned
to Glasnevin. The covering note, from an address in
Mount Merrion read, 'On cleaning out my late husband's
office [d. November 1991] I found this document and
I wondered if you would like to have it'. The document
was a beautifully written commemorative parchment
recording the laying of the foundation stone and the
attendance of dignitaries at the 1939 ceremony.[2] Leading
the attendance were the President of Ireland, Douglas
Hyde, and Eamon de Valera, president of the Executive
Council and Minster for Education and Foreign Affairs,
with prominent members of his government. The minsters
present included: Sean T. O'Kelly (future President);
Frank Aiken, Minister for Coordination of Defence;
Sean Lemass, Minister for Supplies and future Taoiseach;
P.J. Rutledge, Minster for Local Government; Sean
McEntee, Minister for Industry and Commerce; P.J. Little,
Minister for Posts and Telegraphs; Oscar Traynor,
Minister for Defence; Dr Ryan, Minister for Agriculture;
T. Derring, Minister for Lands and Fisheries. The only

woman named was the Lord Mayor, Mrs Clarke, widow
of Tom Clarke, signatory to the 1916 Proclamation and
executed leader of the 1916 Rising. Mrs Clarke, Kathleen,
was Lord Mayor of Dublin from 1939 to 1941.[3] The high
turnout of ministers of the Fianna Fáil government
was probably due to P.J. Munden's close association
with the republican movement. His obituary in *The
Irish Times* records that he had been a member of the
Irish Volunteers, was involved in the Howth gunrunning
of 1914 and, although not 'out' in 1916 was nevertheless
arrested and held in Dublin Castle.[4] Munden continued
his political interest, becoming a founder member and
Hon. Treasurer, in 1948, of the St Stephen's Green branch
of Clann na Poblachta.[5] The chief justice, T. O'Sullivan,
led a representation of fifteen members of the judiciary
drawn from the supreme court, the high court, and the
circuit and district courts of Dublin.[6] Also present were
Mr G. Shannon, chief commissioner of police and representatives of the Dublin Port and Docks. His attendance,
no doubt, marked Munden's long tenure as a member and
chairman of the Dublin Port and Docks Board.

The new, south-facing school building was of impressive
dimensions: 180ft in length and rising to a height of 56ft.
The building was welcomed as 'a refreshing example of
a return to brick', which material was used throughout
in the walls; red courtown for the facing, and a backing
of Tinode bricks. The brickwork was broken only by a
stone cornice. The stonework dressings are of chiselled
County Dublin granite from Thomas Murphy & Sons'
quarries at Sandyford, a company founded in 1890 and
still operating its granite quarry at Barnacullia, Sandyford
in Dublin. In 1939, Munden had completed an oratory

St Mary's Secondary School, designed by W.J. Munden.

for Holy Faith, the Coombe, which, the *Freeman's Journal* reported, was made entirely from Irish materials with Ballinphellic brick and County Dublin granite dressings.[7] The design of the new Glasnevin school was plain, its main feature being the three rows of well-proportioned windows. Floors were of suspended hollow reinforced concrete with a surface of polished woodblock.[8] The ground floor was given over to administration, reception, dining hall, kitchen, and classrooms. On the first floor was a large study hall, library, music rooms, oratory, classrooms, and on the top floor were dormitories, cubicles and tiled bathrooms. The bathrooms were heated and a lift installed. Another practical feature was the infirmary, which was approached from its own staircase, thus facilitating the isolation of patients with infectious conditions. Befitting the times, early 1941, compartments on the ground floor, at the eastern end of the school, were adaptable for use as air-raid shelters.

A NEW NOVITIATE

Building a new novitiate was a stop-go affair. First mooted in 1940, plans were drawn up by Patrick Munden. The 1940 plans show a handsome red-brick building continuing the language of the abutting Georgian house, particularly in the elegant fenestration. The front elevation shows three stories of three bays, a hall door at the extreme left, with three windows above giving an interior mezzanine. The ground floor was given over to the dining rooms, kitchen and ancillary rooms, and the laundry. The first floor provided a large study hall, a smaller study room, one large classroom and two smaller ones, an infirmary with isolation room and two dormitories, one six-bedded and one three-bedded. The top floor was devoted to sleeping accommodation for twenty-nine people over four dormitories, with the addition of two slightly larger bedrooms. The sleeping accommodation was supplemented by three dormitories on the mezzanine giving thirteen beds, a larger bedroom, and a linen room, while an infirmary annex offered a five-bed dormitory. In total there was provision for fifty-six novices with an additional three separate, small bedrooms.[9]

For unknown reasons, and although the plan was approved by the Congregational leadership, the building was not erected and the matter lay dormant until thirteen years later, when it was decided to build a new novitiate without delay. There was a high degree of respect and regard between Munden and the Holy Faith sisters based on an association already thirty years old. Writing to Mother Monica McSherry, Munden reported on a recent illness which had kept him out of circulation for a while: 'I went out too soon and had to stop in bed for the last few days but I expect to be back in the office in a day or two.'[10] In 1955 Munden produced plans for a another impressive, three-storey, red-brick building which, like its unbuilt forerunner, would have complemented the older Georgian house. It was set at an angle of forty-five degrees to the main convent and was to sleep fifty novices but again construction never started.[11]

This time one can speculate on the cause. The 1950s was the period of the congregation's highest rate of expansion outside Ireland, particularly in California and New Zealand, with more houses and schools opening in Trinidad. The leadership of the congregation was inundated with requests from the US to staff parochial schools for the new suburbs mushrooming in the larger cities of the US as part of the post-war baby boom. Archbishop McQuaid was very keen for the Holy Faith sisters to take up many of these invitations and he actively encouraged Mother Monica McSherry in these pioneering undertakings. Of the new school in Norwalk, a suburb of Los Angeles, in 1953, he wrote, 'I trust the enterprise will be a success', and of the expansion to Holy Spirit, Fairfield, in the Diocese of Sacramento, he wrote, 'I consider Holy Spirit an advantage'. McQuaid was particularly enthusiastic about the congregation's venturing to the Antipodes. The 1953 decision to go to Christchurch, New Zealand, 'gives me great pleasure', and four years later, of the move to Auckland and to Australia, he revealed his own part in the decision, 'these Apostolates will have a great development', and he went on to thank Mother Monica for 'listening patiently to my urging'.[12]

At the same time as it was expanding outside Ireland, the congregation was borrowing heavily to meet the need for new schools in Dublin and Kildare, and the two undertakings left little money for a new novitiate in Ireland. Correspondence between Archbishop McQuaid and Mother Monica McSherry shows the rate of expansion and expenditure for schools in Ireland. At that time permission to borrow money had to be obtained from the Holy See through the Archbishop of Dublin and the letter of request had to state the total debt of the Congregation at that time. In 1951, the total debt was £40,000. By 1957 it had more than trebled. Early in 1952 Archbishop McQuaid had just completed a pastoral visitation of Clontarf and wrote to Mother Monica, 'it seems a very grave pity that you would not complete the works in your school in Clontarf'. In response to the archbishop's urging, she referred to the difficult financial situation, but undertook to ask the builder to complete the works. A sum of £21,000 was borrowed immediately to comply with the archbishop's wishes.[13]

In 1953, with the permission of the archbishop, the Holy Faith sisters took on the new school for girls and infants in Finglas East, for which £62,750 was borrowed. Two years later, in two separate tranches, £15,000 and £30,000 was borrowed for St Wolston's, then a secondary school just outside Celbridge, County Kildare. In 1957, £5,000 more was borrowed for St Wolston's and £15,000 for the school at Finglas West. The debt stood at £171,888, perilously close to the overdraft limit of £195,000 set by the bank.[14] The year 1958 opened with yet another substantial loan of £17,500 for the new primary schools in the parish of Glasnevin.

Borrowing continued into the 1960s with £65,000 for schools, including £25,000 for the assembly hall in Glasnevin. Although the principal was being reduced gradually, Irish banks were assessing the risk adversely and in 1966 Archbishop McQuaid agreed to ask the Bank of Nova Scotia to lend £40,000 for Newtownmountkennedy School.[15]

It was, then, a brave decision by Mother Monica to go ahead with the new novitiate in 1968 for which she had to borrow £60,000.[16] With Patrick Munden now deceased, Mother Monica turned to the architectural firm of Tyndall, Hogan & Hurley, who accepted the commission for the design of the new novitiate building.[17] In this design, severely constrained by the finance available, but to the eternal gratitude of future novices, small single rooms replaced the dormitories of the 1955 plans. The estimates of the project cost, £86,000, were submitted on 28 November 1968 but, a mere six weeks later, Richard Hurley advised Mother Monica that mechanical and electrical costs would rise and a likely 5 per cent increase in the cost of materials would result in a tender figure between £90,000 and £95,000.[18] Tenders were received early in the following year, on 6 February 1969, and, as Hurley had predicted, all six tenders reached the £90,000 mark with three exceeding £95,000. The lowest of the six tenders, from Murphy Brothers Ltd of Castlewood Avenue, Dublin 6, was accepted and Murphy Brothers was appointed, with Thomas Garland as consulting engineers and Gerard Larchet overseeing mechanical and electrical Installations.

Building was to commence 1 March 1969 but something happened to delay matters. It appears that the delay was on the Holy Faith side, as a letter from Hurley to Mother Monica McSherry, dated 8 May 1969, refers to 'your recent telephone call informing me of your decision to proceed with the building of the novitiate'.[19] Hurley advised that the delay had affected the general works program of the contractor, but a completion date of September 1970 or a little earlier might be expected. Delays in building usually result in increased costs, and as a result of the Federation of Builders and Trade Unions' negotiated agreement on increased wages, coupled with the inevitable rising costs of materials, £10,000 was added to the total construction cost.

MARIAN HOUSE

In 1989, consultation throughout the congregation on the care of older sisters resulted in a decision in the following year to construct a retirement facility in Glasnevin for sisters in need of care. Initially the plan was to convert the ground floor of the main convent, but in the end the new residential care centre was a conversion of the ground and first floors of the three-storey novitiate. The architect was Stephen Tierney Associates with Matthew Wallace Ltd appointed as the contractor. Named Marian House, the new facility was opened on 8 September 1991, the date traditionally celebrated as Our Lady's birthday. Fewer than ten years had elapsed before it became evident that the capacity of the nursing home would have to be increased. The conversion of the top floor of Marian House, the third storey of the novitiate, was considered, but it was decided to construct a new purpose-built semi-circular building which would more easily allow for the special requirements of a nursing home. The extension was erected partly on an area of land formerly known as Hillside, the freehold interest of which had been conveyed to the congregation in 1943. Stephen Tierney was the architect for the extension, this time with Bradco as the contractors. On 8 July 1998 the clearing of the vegetable garden known as 'Barry's Garden' began. In November the archaeological report arrived confirming that nothing of archaeological interest had been found which would prevent the building going forward. This was the dig carried out by O'Brien, during which the fourteenth-century tile fragment was uncovered. The new extension was blessed by Bishop Moriarty, an Auxiliary Bishop of Dublin, in June 1999. In 2014 Marian House is a HIQA registered nursing home.

A stained-glass window was brought up from St Wolston's to be installed in Marian House prayer room. It had been donated many years earlier by Sr Conleth's parents for the chapel at the former Holy Faith Convent, Ashley, in Clyde Road, Ballsbridge. A description of the window in the chapel in Ashley records its situation at the right of the heavily panelled door and its depiction of the Annunciation, remarkable for its 'rich colours of red and orange'. The window was removed to St Wolston's, County Kildare, in 1942.[20]

Other activity on the site around this time involved the convent in a very minor way. In October 2000, planning permission was granted for the conversion of the single-storey dairy building into small reception rooms and the refurbishment of existing staff facilities. By far the greater part of building activity was associated with the secondary school, including a state-of-the-art all-weather hockey pitch, which, in addition to being used by the school, is licensed to a community group, the Botanic Hockey Club.

THE NEW CENTRE

Today Glasnevin convent site is a multipurpose site serving several generations. The educational mission is served through St Brigid's Primary School, St Mary's Secondary School, and St John's Education Centre, the latter in collaboration with the de la Salle Brothers and many volunteers. Aylward House, formerly St Brigid's Primary School, was adapted in 2000 to provide offices for the central administration of the congregation. The main convent provides a home for a community of almost forty sisters and houses the congregational archives. There further services are provided for the wider community in the form of prayer groups, parenting groups, gatherings of associates and past-pupils. The 1874 dairy has been converted as described above and the original stables remain. Marian House provides residential care for sisters and members of the public.

In deciding to build the new centre, the sisters wanted to share the beauty of their grounds with the local community. They have appropriated the spirit and words of the Sacred Heart sisters who, on leaving Glasnevin, expressed their delight that the site would continue to be

An aerial view of site today. The new centre can clearly be seen.

'a centre and home for the people of Glasnevin'. Just as Margaret Aylward capitalised on the natural beauty of the surroundings and the monastic tradition associated with St Mobhi, so the sisters today wish to draw on that spiritual capital to share their charism in the spirit of inclusivity in contemporary Ireland.

A feature of early Irish monasticism was the monks' affinity with nature in a spirit of respect for God's creation. An image in the centre captures the idea of *viriditas*, a concept central to the thinking of the late medieval saint Hildegard of Bingen, now a doctor of the Church. *Viriditas* is more than mere greenness; it connotes freshness and fruitfulness, growth and vitality. Hildegard saw it as an attribute of divine nature and believed that creation itself would not have been possible without *viriditas*.

The centre will facilitate those seeking short periods of tranquillity by enjoying a solitary walk or the views. Within the centre the framing of views of the lawn and tree canopy in strategically placed almost floor-to-ceiling windows ensures that those of limited mobility will be enabled to enjoy the views. It is hoped that a future development will see interpretive panels explaining the features of botanical and horticultural interest on the walks.

Some years ago, a committee composed of the lay principal of a former Holy Faith school, a lay associate and a sister requested that the sisters offer staff inservice opportunities and workshops for students to become acquainted with the faith and justice heritage of the congregation. Thus the centre will serve as a resource place for sisters and others involved in Holy Faith schools and ministries for days of reflection, professional development, retreat and meetings.

The wider community of parishes, Holy Faith school communities and other groups are welcomed to the facility to participate in programs, events and meetings. Individuals and groups can enjoy quiet times of spiritual reflection and refreshment.

The cedar of Lebanon in the convent grounds, framed in one of the window views from the centre, resonates deeply with the three major world religions of Christianity, Judaism and Islam, and is a compelling symbol for the centre as a privileged place of ecumenical and inter-religious dialogue. Although the historic links between the convent site and the Church of Ireland were strongly represented in the person of Bishop Lindsay, there is room for greater development in ecumenical relations in the twenty-first century and it is hoped that the centre will play a part in fostering dialogue between Christians of all denominations.

In response to the pluralistic and multi-faith society of modern Ireland, the centre will offer a space for inter-religious dialogue involving word and action, and the exploration of different faiths in an atmosphere of respectful listening, along with collaborative action in the fields of social justice and other areas of mutual interest. Inter-religious dialogue is a proven means of fostering social cohesion and cultural harmony.

MOLA Architecture, under lead architect Ralph Bingham, assisted by Kieran Fitzgerald, accepted the commission for the new centre, with Glenbeigh Construction as the main contractors. The project was managed by W.K. Nowlan & Associates, with Henley Kavanagh McGowan as quantity surveyors, DBFL as consulting engineers and Johnson Reid & Associates as the mechanical and electrical engineers.

Margaret Aylward Centre for Faith and Dialogue.

If life is a journey, then the route seldom adopts a linear trajectory, it meanders from place to place. This place is a point of rest, reflection, dialogue, community for all on life's journey. In the spirit of inclusivity and hospitality, all will be welcomed to the centre which is aptly named the Margaret Aylward Centre for Faith and Dialogue.

Afterword

Holy Faith: Lantern in a City Oasis

By Ralph Bingham,
MOLA Architecture

When St Mobhi decided on Glasnevin to found his monastic home some 1,500 years ago, he selected a site that was strategically located on an elevated south-facing slope near the banks of the Tolka river. More importantly he selected a site outside the city boundary, one that overlooked its skyline and was isolated from its sometimes squalid conditions.

Today the Holy Faith landscape is unique, an oasis of tranquillity that has been shaped and formed through the foresight of its benefactors. It is in this context that we find ourselves as architects having the unique privilege and challenge of designing a centre in what Margaret Aylward described 'as a spot fashioned by the Almighty architect of religious ercises'. No pressure so!

In designing the new centre we were very mindful of being respectful to the original eighteenth-century landscape and protected structure of Glasnevin House and associated buildings. We were particularly conscious of the vistas and views from the site and the pristine green lawn and yew walk in front of Glasnevin House. We wanted the new centre to float above this fabulous green carpet as it majestically flows down to the banks of the Tolka.

It was also our intention that the new building should sit as a pavilion or folly within its classical setting and should appear weightless as an object building. To minimise its impact it was decided to depart from the use of brick, as used in the existing necklace of institutional buildings, but to instead use opaque glass panels to mirror its glorious surroundings. The external skin will thus reflect the trees, sky, lawn and convent buildings around it.

The plan of the centre represents a journey of discovery, a spiral and labyrinth. It is formed from a series of axial circulation routes which are geometrically formed to contain space. These spaces operate as a theatre, a sacred space, a multipurpose space and a series of small office-size rooms, all linked and interlocked with ramps and steps. The central theatre space is a double-height volume, forming the fulcrum of the plan and acting as a forum for major gatherings. The space contains a kitchenette and can be used for dining or as a space for talks, classes and activity-based programs.

Although a relatively small building, it is complex in both section and plan as it steps down the hill and maximises the spectacular vistas and views. For example, the main staircase that rises up to the sacred space is on axis with Mitchell's Lebanese cedar tree. The steps down to the theatre space are in line with the O'Connell tower and tree tops of Glasnevin cemetery. The view from the large curved window in the first-floor sacred space acts as a lens over the city skyline. A large roof terrace provides a breakout area from the sacred space and as a further place of contemplation.

Pavilions are traditionally simple forms, and part of our challenge was to organise and represent all the separate brief agendas as a unified object. Making a form look simple is often a difficult and rigorous process. The sacred space is elliptical in plan and provides a soft natural counterpoint to the angular walls that lightly envelope it.

While the exterior of the building is unapologetically contemporary, with a neutral colour palette of greys and whites, the interior comprises natural materials of timber wall linings, stone and oak flooring. Marmoluem, made from linseed oil and jute, is used on circulation routes. The new centre is designed with best practice in sustainability in mind and is airtight, well insulated and benefits from heat recovery. Solar panels on the roof of the sacred space assist in the heating of hot water, while underfloor heating provides good background warmth within the centre. A green sedum roof provides an additional layer of insulation, whilst also improving water attenuation and giving a fifth elevation when viewed from the upper floors of the convent and Glasnevin House.

With a bespoke building with no previous prototypes, there is always an anxiety about whether the reality matches the vision. The context of the site warrants high aspirations and one that hopefully can be delivered and exceeded. It is a collective effort and any building is only as good as its ingredients – its brief, its client, the site, the design team, the contractor and their team of sub-contractors and craftsmen. At this point we would like to commend the belief, bravery and commitment shown by all parties involved in the project.

Like Margaret Aylward, the current Sisters of the Holy Faith congregation, have left a legacy and gift for future generations and one that will act as a lantern in this wonderful city oasis.

NOTES

1
MOBHI TO MITCHELL

1 F. Erlington Ball, *A History of the County Dublin: the people, parishes and antiquities from the earliest time to the close of the eighteenth century*, vol. 6 (Dublin: Alex Thom, 1920), 124.

2 HFA/SBO/9AR/16 December 1865/18–21.

3 Judith Carroll, Excavations, 1996: 123; Mary McMahon, Excavations 1989: 24; 1990: 36; 2002: 541; 2003: 533; Helen Keogh, Excavations, 2005: 123, www.excavations.ie.

4 Richard N. O'Brien, *Archaeological Monitoring at Holy Faith Convent, Old Finglas Rd., Glasnevin, Dublin*, 11, August 1998, www.excavations.ie, 98E0299, also in HFA/GF/ED/28A/45.

5 *A Survey of Part of the Land of Glasnevin in the County of Dublin for George Putland Esquire containing 22 acres*, November 1799, NLI, ms. map, 16G.41 (18); Liam Clare, 'The Putland Family of Dublin and Bray,' *Dublin Historical Review*, 54, 2, Autumn (2001): 183–209; Neil O'Flanagan, Excavations 2001: 423 and 424; Rosanne Meenan, Excavations, 1996: 124 at www.excavations.ie.

6 Franc Myles, *Archaeological Assessment Report for a proposed development at Holy Faith Convent, Glasnevin Demesne, Glasnevin, Dublin*, 11, 2010, 2–10, Aylward House, Glasnevin.

7 Myles, *Archaeological Assessment*, 2010, 8, 9.

8   Amanda Kearney, 'Homeland Emotion: An Emotional Geography of Heritage and Homeland', *International Journal of Heritage Studies*, 15 (2-3, 2009), 211.

9   James Mills (ed.), *Account Roll of the Priory of the Holy Trinity, Dublin, 1337–1346* (Dublin: Four Courts Press, 1996), ix, x.

10   Mills, *Account Roll*, Appendix, 189, 191.

11   Ball, *A History of the County Dublin*, 124.

12   Michael O'Neill, 'Christ Church Cathedral and its Environs: Medieval and Beyond,' in *Medieval Dublin X, Proceedings of the Friends of Medieval Dublin Symposium*, Sean Duffy (ed.) (Dublin: Four Courts Press, 2009), 298–321.

13   A Map of part of the lands of Glasnevin part of the Estate of the Dean of Christ Church held by John Bayly, copied from a survey made by Richard Francis in the year 1640 and traced out by Thomas Cave in the year 1730. By a scale of 20 Perches to an Inch, National Library of Ireland, online at http://catalogue.nli. ie/Record/vtls000301157; Robert C. Simington (ed.), *The Civil Survey AD 1654–1656, vol II of the County of Dublin* (Dublin: Irish Manuscripts Commission, 1945), 182.

14   Tony O'Doherty, *A History of Glasnevin* (Dublin: Original Writing, 2011), 44, 45.

15   ROD, 306-284-263359.

16   www.measuringworth.com.

17   ROD 76-445-55300; Clare, 'The Putland Family,' 183–209.

18   Survey for George Putland, NLI, ms. map, 16G.41 (18).

19   Ball, *A History of the County Dublin*, 148; John Angel, *A General History of Ireland in its Ancient and Modern State* (Dublin: printed for the author, 1781), 252.

20   The Knight of Glin and James Peill, *Irish Furniture* (Yale: Yale University Press, 2007), 95.

21   Finola O'Kane, *Landscape Gardening in Eighteenth-Century Ireland: Mixing Foreign Trees with the Natives* (Cork: Cork University Press, 2004), 3.

22   Angelique Day (ed.), *Letters from Georgian Ireland, the Correspondence of Mary Delany, 1731–68* (Dublin: The Friar Bush Press, 1991), 40; M. Laird and A. Weinberg-Roberts, *Mrs Delany and Her Circle* (Yale: Yale University Press, 2009), 8.

23   *The Evergreen Grove at Delville with Dublin Bay in the Distance*, 1747, Ink, graphite and wash on paper, 25.2 x 36.4 cm, NGI.2722.22; E. Charles Nelson and Eileen M. McCracken, *The Brightest Jewel: A History of the National Botanic Gardens Glasnevin* (Kilkenny: Boethius, 1987), 43, fig. 22; Finola O'Kane, 'The Appearance of a Continued City: Dublin's

Georgian suburbia,' in *Georgian Dublin*, Gillian O'Brien et al. (eds) (Dublin: Four Courts Press, 2008), 121.

24 Day, *Letters from Georgian Ireland*, 12 July 1774; Edward Malins and the Knight of Glin, *Lost Demesnes, Irish Landscape Gardening* 1660–1845 (London: Barrie & Jenkins, 1976), 37; M. Laird and A. Weinberg-Roberts, *Mrs Delany and Her Circle*, 6; C.P. Curran, *Dublin Decorative Plasterwork in the Eighteenth and Nineteenth Centuries* (London: Alec Tiranti, 1967), 21, Plates 10 and 11.

25 Nelson and McCracken, *Brightest Jewel*, 44.

26 O'Doherty, *Glasnevin*, 69; M. Laird and A. Weinberg-Roberts, *Mrs Delany and Her Circle*, 8.

27 *A View of Beggar's Hut in the Garden of Deville, Dublin, 1745*, NGI, 2722.23; *The Evergreen Grove at Delville with Dublin Bay in the Distance*, NGI, 2722.22; *The Cold Bath Field at Delville*, NGI, 2722.43; *A View of Swift and Swans Island*, NGI, 2722.44.

28 'On the Sale of Delville Glasnevin Home of Mrs Delany,' *The Irish Book Lover*, XIV (January 1924), 11.

29 Day, *Letters from Georgian Ireland*, 19 January 1750, 49.

30 M. Bence Jones, *A Guide to Irish Country Houses* (London: Constable, revised second edition, 1988), 135.

31 Susan Roundtree, 'Dublin Bricks and Brickmakers,' *Dublin Historical Record* 60, 1 (Spring, 2007), 65.

32 Maurice Craig, 'The Quest for Sir Edward Lovett Pearce,' *Irish Arts Review*, 12 (1996) 30–34; Jeremy Williams, 'The Elusive Sir Edward Lovett Pearce,' *Irish Arts Review*, 1 (2001), 100 and 100 n.6.

33 Williams, 'Elusive Sir Edward', 100.

34 Margaret Gaughren, *History of the Congregation*, HFA/HC/S/21/16.

35 Quoted in 'Windows: A Guide to the Repair of Historic Windows', text by Nessa Roche (Department of the Environment, Heritage and Local Government: 2007), 10.

36 The Knight of Glin, *Irish Furniture*, 95.

37 Andrea Marrinan, 'Glasnevin House: Its Occupants, Builders, Architecture and Principal Plasterwork Schemes' (BA thesis, Trinity College Dublin, 1911), 45–47.

38 Joseph McDonnell, 'Patrons and Plasterers: The Origin of Dublin Rococo Stuccowork,' in *The Eighteenth Century Town House: form, function, finance*, Christine Casey (eds) (Dublin: Four Courts Press, 2012), 226; Marrinan, 'Glasnevin House', 48, 49.

39 Curran, *Dublin Decorative Plasterwork*, 21.

40 The Knight of Glin and James Peill, *Irish Furniture*, 2007, 95.

41 Edward McParland review of Joseph McDonald, 'Irish Eighteenth

Century Stuccowork and its European Origins' in *Irish Arts Review Yearbook*, 1991, 259.

42 Marrinan, 'Glasnevin House', 55.

43 McDonnell, 'Patrons and Plasterers', 226 and 'Continental Stuccowork and English Rococo Carving at Russborough', in *Irish Architecture and Decorative Studies, Journal of the Irish Georgian Society*, 14 (2011), 114.

44 O'Doherty, *Glasnevin*, 155.

45 *Little Sketch of the Early Days of the Congregation of the Holy Faith*, n.d., HFA/HC/S/21/2A.

46 Ruth McManus, *Dublin 1910–1940: Shaping the City and its Suburbs* (Dublin: Four Courts Press, 2002), 385–387. Robert Douglas Strain was aged 65 in the 1911 census.

2
LINDSAY FAMILY AND SACRED HEART SISTERS

---

1 'The Story of Glasgow University', http://universitystory.gla.ac.uk/biography.

2 http://www.thepeerage.com/p2047.htm#i20469.

3 James Frost, *The History and Topography of the County of Clare, List of the Protestant Bishops of Killaloe* (Dublin: Sealy, Brynes and Walker, 1893), www.clarelibrary.ie/eolas/coclare/chap10_killaloe_protestant_bishops.htm

4 Kenneth Milne, *Christ Church Cathedral Dublin* (Dublin: Four Courts Press, 2000), 291.

5 Anna Moran, 'Merchants and Material Culture in 19th Century Dublin', *Irish Architecture and Decorative Studies* XI (2008), 146–148.

6 Walter Strickland, *A Dictionary of Irish Artists* (Cambridge: Cambridge University Press, 1913 reprint 2012), 25. The query referred to a pamphlet in the National Library containing a 'short poem in explanation of designs drawn and painted for the Board (or Reception) Room of the Irish Harp Society's House in Glasnevin, by Miss E.H. Trotter, to illustrate the revival etc of music,' *The Irish Book Lover*, XVIII (Jan–Feb 1930), 25.

7 Nelson and McCracken, *Brightest Jewel*, 59.

8 http://churchrecords.irishgenealogy.ie, DU-CI-MA-913.

9 O'Doherty, *Glasnevin*, 61–65.

10 Letter from Charles Lindsay to William H. Gregory, Undersecretary of Ireland, 16 February 1819, NAI/CSO/RP/1819/504.

11 Fever Report of Board of Health for district of Finglas and
    Glasnevin, County Dublin, for the period 23 September to
    1 October 1820, NAI/CSO/RP/1820/1609.

12 Letter from Charles Lindsay to William H. Gregory, Undersecretary
    of Ireland, 1818, NAI/ CSO/RP/1818/375; letter from Charles
    Lindsay to Charles Grant, Chief Secretary, Irish Office, London,
    NAI/CSO/RP/1819/549.

13 Kenneth Milne, *Christ Church Cathedral*, 287–290.

14 O'Doherty, *Glasnevin*, 150.

15 www.churchrecords.ie, DU-CI-MA-66161;
    www.titheapplotmentbooks/Dublin/Glasnevin/TheTurrets;
    O'Doherty, *Glasnevin*, 95.

16 Kenneth Milne, *Christ Church Cathedral*, 316–318.

17 Dublin Union of Clontarf, Return by the Revd W. Walsh,
    DDA/AB3/32/3/44/1.

18 www.titheapplotmentbooks,NAI/Dublin/GlasnevinHouse/Demesne.

19 Notice from Glasnevin House, 6 April 1840, DDA/AB3/32/3/137/1.

20 Nelson and McCracken, *Brightest Jewel*, 42, figs. 20, 21.

21 ibid., 156.

22 ibid., 175.

23 O'Doherty, *Glasnevin*, 97.

24 Will of Charles Lindsay Bishop of Kildare, Probate Court
    of Canterbury, National Archives of United Kingdom,
    PROB II/2216/344; the will with its two codicils was granted
    probate in 1855; http://Churchrecords.ie, DU-CI-BU-13025.

25 www.churchrecords.ie DU-CI-BU-1025.

26 Letter M. Dunne to Dr Murray, Archbishop of Dublin,
    DDA/AB3/32/3/137/1.

27 George Lindsay, NAI/RLFC/3/1/120.

28 Glasnevin: First House of the Society of the Sacred Heart in Dublin,
    MAV/20 (1).

29 Glasnevin: First House, MAV/20 (1).

30 ibid.

31 Memorial of Indenture of a Lease, 23 September 1863, George
    Hayward Lindsay, Venerable Charles Lindsay, Henry Lindsay and
    others to Thomas Scully, ROD, 1853-26-57; for Julia Scully as superior
    in *Glasnevin Journal de la Maison du Sacre Coeur de Dublin fondée en Octobre
    1853*, entry for 27 January 1865, MAV/93 (1).

32 *Journal de la Maison*, entry for 23 October 1953, MAV/93 (1);
    In Ireland the Lazarists were known as the Vincentians or members
    of the Congregation of the Mission, CM.

33 Lettres Annuels 1859–1861; Glasnevin: First House, MAV/20 (1).

34 Glasnevin: First House, MAV/20 (1); Lettres Annuels 1859–1861.

35 Julia Scully to Cardinal Cullen, 28 March 1863,
    DDA/AB4/340/9/1/33.

36 *Freeman's Journal*, 26 August 1911.

37 *Journal de la Maison*, entry for 26 July 1865, MAV/93 (i).

38 Rose Gaughren, *History of the Congregation*, HFA/HC/S/21/16.

39 *Journal de la Maison*, entry for 27 September 1865, MAV/93/1,
    Mortuary Register, MAV/95 (1).

40 Glasnevin: First House, MAV/20 (1).

41 Jacinta Prunty, *Margaret Aylward: Lady of Charity, Sister of Faith
    1810–1889* (Dublin: Four Courts Press, 1999), 22–37.

42 Prunty, *Margaret Aylward*, 56–59.

43 Anne-Marie Close, 'A Meeting of Minds?': Margaret Aylward and
    Paul Cullen' in *Cardinal Paul Cullen and His World*, Dáire Keogh and
    Albert McDonnell (eds) (Dublin: Four Courts Press, 2011), 221–229.

44 Gaughren, *History*, HFA/HC/S/21/16.

45 HFA/MA/F/01/77.

46 HFA/MA/F/01/63A, n.d.

3

HOLY FAITH SISTERS
IN GLASNEVIN HOUSE

1 *Little Sketch of the Early Days*, HFA/HC/S/21/2A.

2 ROD, 1865-29-140.

3 Prunty, *Margaret Aylward*, 122.

4 HFA/SBO/15AR/ 1872/15.

5 *Little Sketch of the Early Days*, HFA/HC/S/21/2A.

6 DDA/AB8/ advertisement is unattributed.

7 Boarding School Cash Book 1874, HFA/GA/CSI/BS/1, 2.

8 Boarding School Cash Book, March, 1873, HFA/GA/CSI/BS/1, 2.

9 Boarding School Cash Book, April 1876, HFA/GA/CSI/BS/1, 2.

10 *Freeman's Journal*, 20 August 1874, 5.

11 ibid., 3 September, 1900, 15.

12 Margaret Aylward to Dr Kirby, dated 30 October 1864,
    HFA/Mc/K/12/28.

13 HFA/SBO/9AR/1865/21.

14 Letter dated 31 September 1866, DDA/AB5/VI/ 327/6/ 16.

15 HFA/SBO/15AR/1872/15–16.

16 Prunty, *Margaret Aylward*, 109.
17 HFA/ GA/MA/F/01/63.
18 HFA/GA/ C/31/2/ 1a.
19 HFA/SBO, 21AR, 1877, 14.
20 HFA/SBO, 21AR, 1877, 14.

4

CONVENT CHAPEL: CONSTRUCTION, LITURGICAL FURNITURE AND DECORATION

1 I am indebted to Sr Therese Kearney CHF for her identification of contractors and payments for the building and decoration of the convent chapel, 2011, HFA, Display.
2 DIA, entry for W.H. Byrne, online version, www.dia.ie.
3 Plans for Glasnevin chapel in W.H. Byrne Collection, IARC/2006/142 (POO 194); entry for W.H. Byrne, DIA, online version, www.dia.ie.
4 www.census.nationalarchives.ie: 1901/Kiernan/James/Dublin/ Clontarf/East/VictoriaTerrace; 1911/Kiernan/James/Dublin/ Blackrock/No1/BooterstownAvenue; *IB* 12 February 1903.
5 Cash Book 1900, entry dated 4 August and 25 October; Cash Book, 1901, entry dated 11 February and 25 April, HFA/CS1/ 1.
6 DIA, entry for E. Sharp, www.dia.ie; *IB* 46, 18 June 1904, 372; Dublin Historic Industry Database, January 2011, 12, www.gsi.ie.
7 *IB* 46, 18 June 1904, 372.
8 Edmund Sharp, Publicity Pamphlet, Sculptor, 42 Pearse St Dublin, 9, 10.
9 DIA, entry for Patrick Tomlin, www.dia.ie
10 E. Sharp, *IB*, vol. 44, 7 May 1903, 17.
11 Obituary for Sharp, *IB*, 72, 11 October 1930, 910.
12 'A Brief History of the Congregation,' n.d. The annotation relating to the high altar is in a different hand from the rest of the document and is dated 1901, HFA/HC/S/21/16.
13 Cash Book, 1901, entry dated 30 August, 4 October; Cash Book 1902, entry dated 18 March, HFA/CS1/1; for brief architectural description of church in Clones see www.clonesparish.com.
14 HFA/GA/H/28/1.
15 www.census.nationalarchives.ie, Dublin/North Dock/ North Strand Road; Cash Book, 1900, entry 17 February 1900 for gilding the altar; entry 10 March 1900 for cemetery work for which

he was paid £2 6s and entry 17 February 1900, 2s for pedestal, HFA/CS1/1.

16 DIA, entry for Beakey, www.dia.ie.

17 Cash Book, 1900, entry dated 21 June to Mr P. Beakey for Clontarf; Cash Book 1901, entry dated 8 March, to Mr Beakey, Stafford St for 20 school desks and one teacher's desk for Clarendon Street, HFA/CS1/1.

18 *IB*, 57, 13 March 1915, 129.

19 DIA, entry for Munden, www.dia.ie.

20 *IB*, 11 October 1913, 655; *IB*, 8 April 1922, 233; *IB*, 20 May, 1922, 356.

21 Centre for Advancement of Women in Politics, www.qub.ac.uk.

22 Paul McKeever, 'The influence of the great French organ-builder Aristide Cavaillé-Coll on the Dublin organ-builder John White: the 1871 organ of St. Andrew's Church, Westland Row as a case study' (paper given at the Joint Annual Conference of the Society for Musicology in Ireland and the Royal Musical Association, Dublin, 2009).

23 DIA, entry for White, www.dia.ie.

24 The Heritage Council, 'The Care of Stained Glass', text by Dr David Lawrence, n.d.

25 www.mayer-of-munich.com; DIA, entry for Mayer, www.dia.ie.

26 DIA, entry for Clarke, Harry, www.dia.ie.

27 Gail Tierney, 'Franz Meyer & Company and Zettler Studios', 1995, www.slif-silesstreet.com.

28 David Lawrence, 'Nineteenth Century Stained Glass in the Church of Ireland Diocese of Limerick and Killaloe', *Irish Architecture and Decorative Studies*, 10, 2007, 182.

29 Unus Dominus, Una Fides, S. Patricius, ora pro nobis; Unus Dominus, Una Fides. S. Brigida, ora pro nobis.

5
THE 1901 CENSUS:
VILLAGE AND CONVENT COMMUNITY

1 O'Doherty, *Glasnevin*, 177.

2 Séamas O Maitiú, *Dublin's Surburban Towns 1834–1930* (Dublin: Four Courts Press, 2003), 45.

3 Ruth McManus, *Dublin 1910–1940*, XX; O'Doherty, *Glasnevin*, 116–119.

4 O'Doherty, *Glasnevin*, 98.

5 IAA, Entry for Institute of Industrial Research and Standards.

6 www.census.nationalarchives.ie/1901/Dublin/Glasnevin/Glasnevin; O'Doherty, *Glasnevin*, 99.

7   Landed Estates Database, www.landedestates.nuigalway.ie.

8   O'Doherty, *Glasnevin*, 126.

9   ibid., 231–238;

10 www.census.nationalarchives.ie/1901/Dublin/Glasnevin/
    Church Hill. Naul Road.

11 Mary E. Daly, 'Catholic Dublin: The Public Expression in the Age
    of Paul Cullen', in Keogh and McDonnell (eds), *Paul Cullen*, 138;
    McManus, *Dublin 1910–1940*, 310.

12 www.census.nationalarchives.ie/1901/Dublin/Glasnevin/
    Church Lane.

13 Dublin Historic Industry Database, January 2100, 15, www.gsi.ie.

14 Charles Duggan, Heritage Appraisal Report, Ballymun Road,
    No 12, Glasnevin, Dublin 9 in connection with planning permission
    6092/06, http://dublincity.ie/AnitePublicDocs/000694801.pdf.

15 George W. Craigie, architect, is listed in the Post Office Dublin
    Directory at Merville, Glasnevin, from 1893. A son, Arthur Craigie,
    born in 1888 or 1889, is also described as an architect in the 1911
    census and was a member of the AAI from 1904 until 1909, DIA,
    entry for G. Craigie, www.dia.ie; O'Doherty, Glasnevin, 100.

16 www.cro.ie.

17 www.census.nationalarchives.ie/1901/Dublin/Glasnevin/
    Glasnevin Demesne.

18 HFA/AR/SBO/1897/25.

19 HFA/MA/F/01/69. Nd.

20 Prunty, *Margaret Aylward*, 127–131.

21 *Sisters of the Holy Faith Centenary Book*, 1967, Foreword, HFA, Display.

22 There were 149 persons resident (sisters and pupils). There is a
    discrepancy here since the combined totals of seventy-one sisters in
    the community and seventy-five boarders is three fewer persons than
    the enumerator's figure of 149, www.census.nationalarchives/1901/
    Dublin/Glasnevin/Glasnevin Demesne.

23 HFA/MA/F/01 No. 63A.

24 Prunty, *Margaret Aylward*, 129.

25 Maeve O'Riordain, 'Assuming Control: Elite Women as Household
    Managers in the late Nineteenth Century', in Ciaran O'Neill (ed.),
    Irish Elites in the Nineteenth Century (Dublin: Four Courts Press, 2013)
    83–98.

26 Entry Register HFA.

27 O'Riordan, 'Assuming Control', 95.

28 Gaughren, *History*, HFA/HC/S/21/16; *Little Sketch of the Early Days*,
    HFA/HC/S/21/2A.

29 Convent Cash Book, entry for June 1900 HFA; Dublin Historic Industry Database, January 2100, 12, www.gsi.ie.

30 Statement of Captain Sean Prendergast, Former Officer Commanding 'C' Company, 1st Battalion, Dublin Brigade, Irish Volunteers and Irish Republican Army, www.bureauofmilitaryhistory.ie, BMH/WS/755.

31 Rose Doyle, *Trade Names: Traditional Traders and Shopkeepers of Dublin* (New Island: Dublin, 2004), 53–56.

32 www.cro.ie; Andy Bielenberg, 'A Survey of the Irish Flour Milling industry 1801–1922', Paper for annual Hnag meeting at the ESRI, Friday 31 January, 2003); Doyle, *Trade Names*, 197.

33 www.census.nationalarchives.ie/1901 Dublin/Glasnevin/ Glasnevin Demesne.

6
THE SITE TAKE ITS PRESENT SHAPE

1 P. Munden, Sketch Plan Proposed Boarding School and Young Ladies Hostel, HFA/CS1/BS/1.

2 Parchment with covering note from Dorothy Munden, HFA/GF/ED/28A/17.

3 ibid.

4 *The Irish Times*, 22 March 1962.

5 *Freeman's Journal*, 26 June 1948, 6.

6 HFA/GF/ED/28A/17.

7 www.murphystone.com; *Freeman's Journal*, 21 June 1936.

8 *IB*, 4 Jan 1941 with picture of school.

9 P. Munden, Plans for a proposed new novitiate dated 10 April 1940, HFA/GA/CS1/NOV/1, 2, 3.

10 P.J. Munden to Mother Monica, 24 September 1952, HFA/CS/30/2.

11 Plans for New Novitiate Glasnevin, Munden and Purcell, 1955, Munden Collection, IAA/85/141.149/1-11.

12 McQuaid to Mother Monica, 30 July 1953, DDA/AB8/8B/4; McQuaid to Mother Monica, 13 October 1954, DDA/AB8/8B/4; McQuaid to Mother Monica, 24 August 1953, DDA/AB8/8B/4; McQuaid to Mother Monica, 31 May 1957, DDA/AB8/8B/5.

13 McQuaid to Mother Monica, 27 February 1952; Mother Monica to McQuaid 28 February 1952, DDA/AB8/8B/3.

14 Mother Monica to McQuaid on Finglas school, letter dated 13

March 1953 and 24 March 1953, DDA/AB8/8B/4; Mother Monica to McQuaid on St Wolstons, letter dated 11 June 1955 and 11 October 1955, DDA/AB8/8B/4; Mother Monica to McQuaid on St Wolstons and Finglas West, letter dated 11 June 1957, DDA/AB8/8B/5.

15 Correspondence dated 10 June 1966, DDA/AB8/8B/6.

16 Permission of the Holy See in document signed by Archbishop McQuaid, 2 July 1968, HFA/GF/H/28.

17 Letter from Richard Hurley to Mother Monica McSherry, dated 31 July 1968, HFA, Glasnevin.

18 Letter from Richard Hurley to Mother Monica McSherry, 10 February 1969, HFA, Glasnevin, uncatalogued.

19 Hurley to Mother Monica, 7 October 1969, HFA, uncatalogued.

20 Anonymous account of sisters in St Mary's Road, HFA/CS/14/3.

INDEX

Allingham, Sr Ada, 50, 51, 66, 98
Atley family, 106
Auckland, 115
Australia, 115
Aylward House, 56, 108, 120
Aylward, Lindsay, see Sacred Heart Sisters
Aylward, Margaret,
    Centre Faith & Dialogue, 123, 124
    Extension of convent, 57, 58
    Foundress, 23, 50, 51, 55, 96–8, 101, 128
    Glasnevin purchase, 23, 24, 39, 54
    Glasnevin reflections, 8, 12, 121, 126
    St Brigid's Orphanage, 50, 61
    St Brigid's Schools, 12, 50, 55, 61–9

Beakey, Robert, 79
Bingham, Ralph, 123, 125
Bon Secours Hospital, 8, 9

Botanic Gardens, 16, 35, 42, 91, 92, 94, 110
Byrne, W.H., 29, 72–4, 80

Casciani, Antonio, 78, 79
Christ Church Cathedral, 10, 12, 14, 16, 34, 35, 38
Christchurch, New Zealand, 115
Coussmaker, Eliza, 32
Craigie family, 44, 92, 94, 95
Croft, Mother Eliza, 45, 49
Cullen, Cardinal, 45, 46, 48, 50, 54, 70, 89

De Valera, Eamon, 99, 111
Delany, Mary, 17, 19, 20, 21, 25
Delany, Patrick, 15
Delville, 15, 17–21, 28, 36, 91, 92
Downes Bakery, 103

Fydell, Elizabeth, 32, 36, 43

Glasnevin, Bailiff, 13, 14
Glasnevin Hill 22, 60, 90
Glasnevin Village, 15, 16, 47, 88, 89

St Brigid's National School, 57, 108, 120
St Mary's Secondary School, 57, 81, 82, 84, 108, 110, 113, 120
Glasnevin House, 10, 12, 15–18, Architectural assessment, 21, 24, 25, 30
Plasterwork, 20, 26–9
Gowan, John, 50, 60, 62–4, 68, 72, 78, 96, 98

Holy Trinity Priory, 12
Hurley, Richard, 117, 118
Hyde, Douglas, 111

Kelly, John, 25, 27
Kelly, Mother Elizabeth, 111
Kiernan, James, 29, 74

Lindsay, Archdeacon Charles, 38, 43
Lindsay, Bishop Charles, Administration, 38
Entombed, 92
Marriages, 32
Owner Glasnevin House, 12, 32, 34, 35, 38, 39, 41, 42
Pastoral activity, 36–8
Sacred Heart Sisters, 45
Yew walk, 41, 42
Will, 43
Lindsay, George Haywood, 39, 43, 44, 56
Lindsay, Lt-Col Henry Gore, 39, 82, 92
Los Angeles, 115

Macken, R., 110
Mayer & Co., 83–5

McQuaid, Archbishop, 56, 115–17
McSherry, Mother Monica, 115, 116, 118
Mitchell, Hugh Henry, snr, 10, 11, 15–17, 20, 28, 58, 127
Mobhi, St, 8–11, 65, 90, 92, 121, 126
MOLA Architecture, 123
Mountjoy Brewery, 105
Munden, Patrick, 57, 80, 81, 110–15, 117
Murtagh Bros., 105

Pearce, Edward Lovett, 22, 23, 28
Phillips, Frederick, 82
Putland, George, 14
Putland, John, 14–16

Rogerson, Sir John, 10, 15, 16, 24, 39, 92 104
Ryan, Thos & Co., 28, 29

Sacramento, 115
Sacred Heart Sisters, 23, 45, 48–50, 56, 7, 120
Scully, Julia, 45, 54
Scully, Thomas, 45, 49
Sharp, Edmund, 75–8
Strain, Alexander, 29

Tickell, Thomas 42, 92
Tierney, Stephen 118, 119
Trinidad, Thomas, 115

Vickers, Agnes, 99, 102, 103, 123

White, John, 82, 83

If you enjoyed this book, you may also be interested in…

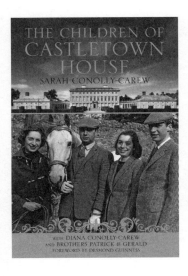

The Children of Castletown House

SARAH CONOLLY-CAREW

Castletown House, in County Kildare, was Ireland's largest private residence, which was once an alternative seat of political power to Dublin. The four Conolly-Carew children were the last generation to grow up within its walls, and their story is a window into Ireland's real Downton Abbey, a world of servants and lavish balls, of cars run on charcoal, visiting Princesses, IRA intimidation and Olympic glory.

978 1 84588 750 6

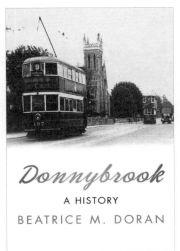

Donnybrook: A History

BEATRICE M. DORAN

Donnybrook is one of the most iconic areas of south county Dublin, a suburban arcadia known for its wide leafy roads and fine houses. But there is more to Donnybrook than that, and in this excellent book Dr Beatrice Doran takes the reader through its long and colourful history from the earliest times to the present day through a series of rare and beautifully produced photographs which show the ever-changing face of Donnybrook.

978 1 84588 769 8